RETURN FROM EXILE

OVERCOMING
Loss, Failure & Personal Setbacks

a spiritual recovery guide by
F. Remy Diederich

All Rights Reserved
No portion of this publication may be reproduced, stored in any electronic system or transmitted in any form or by any means, electronic, mechanical, photocopy, recording or otherwise, without the written permissions from the author and publisher. Brief quotations may be used in literary reviews.

Unless otherwise indicated, all Scripture quotations are taken from the HOLY BIBLE, NEW INTERNATIONAL VERSION, Copyright 1973, 1978, 1984,2011 by Biblica Inc. Used by permission of Zondervan. All rights reserved worldwide.

Scripture taken from the Holy Bible, NEW INTERNATIONAL READER'S VERSION, marked (NIRV) ®.Copyright © 1996, 1998 Biblica. All rights reserved throughout the world. Used by permission of Biblica.

Scripture taken from the New Century Version marked (NCV). Copyright © 1987, 1988, 1991 by Thomas Nelson, Inc. Used by permission. All rights reserved.

Scripture quotations taken from the New American Standard Bible® (NASB),Copyright © 1960, 1962, 1963, 1968, 1971, 1972, 1973,1975, 1977, 1995 by The Lockman Foundation. Used by permission. www.Lockman.org"

Front and back cover graphics by Jason M. Brooks.

Copyright © 2016 F. Remy Diederich
All rights reserved.

ISBN-13: 978-1535001748

ISBN-10: 1535001747

A road-map through the wilderness of loss...

Return from Exile: Overcoming Loss, Failure, & Personal Setbacks is a book for which I have been waiting a long time. It is an honest and authentic exploration of something many Christians are afraid to face: *How do you truly process loss and begin to move forward?* For so long we felt we had to face loss alone and unprepared. Platitudes and Bible verses make sense in our heads, but the pain is in our hearts.

In this book, F. Remy Diederich asks the same hard questions we ask ourselves. Then he offers a safe place to take an honest look at what weighs us down and holds us prisoner. *Return from Exile* is a road-map through the wilderness of loss.

With this 40-day devotional and Remy's personal reflections, you will find you are not alone. I was truly amazed at how a book so small could contain such a large amount of truth, hope, and practical application.

Bobbi Graffunder

To Diedre Kaye:
Thank you for being such an inspiration
to so many people in your exile.

CONTENTS

	Introduction	1
1	How Did I Get Here?	6
2	The Six D's of Exile	11
3	Five Reasons for Ending Up in Exile	15
4	Laid Bare	20
5	Exile is Everywhere	23
6	I Didn't See This Coming!	27
7	Embracing Your Dark Side	32
8	Eight Types of Exile	36
9	Experiencing Loss	41
10	Denying Your Loss	44
11	Journaling Your Exile	48
12	Secondary Losses	51
13	Invalidation	55
14	Limited Choices	59
15	Personal Trauma	63
16	Bittersweet	67
17	Unmet Needs	70
18	Traveling Companions	74
19	Lamentation	78
20	Comfort in Exile	82
21	Scattered Shame	85
22	Exile Wisdom	90
23	The Two Halves of Life	94
24	The Enemy of the Good	98
25	The Discipline of Darkness	102
26	Facing Your Nakedness	106
27	Return from Exile	109
28	Grieve Your Loss	112
29	Listen	116
30	Admit	119
31	Face Your Shame	122
32	Peace in the Pain	126
33	Be the Hero	130

34	Reframing the Loss	135
35	Reframing Your Offender	138
36	Reframing Your Identity	142
37	Reframing God	146
38	Necessary Endings	150
39	Double Blessings	153
40	Goodness and Mercy	157
	Epilogue	163
	Appendix: The Gift of Cancer	165
	A Word from the Author	168
	Other Books by the Author	169
	Acknowledgments	170
	About the Author	171
	Endnotes	172

Other books by F. Remy Diederich

- Healing the Hurts of Your Past... *a guide to overcoming the pain of shame.*

- STUCK...*how to overcome your anger and reclaim your life.*

- Out of Exile...*a forty-day journey from setback to comeback.* (Pastor's Edition)

Exile:

A prolonged separation from one's country or home, as by force of circumstances.[1]

Introduction

*Exile is when life throws you a curveball and
you end up in a place you never thought you would be.*

A few years ago I spoke at a pastors retreat on the theme of exile. That might seem like an odd topic, but much of the Bible is written to God's people about exile: how to avoid it, how to live in it, and how to successfully return from it.

What is exile? Exile is when life throws you a curveball and you end up in a place you never thought you would be: divorced, depressed, abused, bankrupt, fired, disabled, abandoned, etc.

You feel stuck, like a beached whale, with no way back. Exile convinces you that life will never be good again and so you resign yourself to a second-class existence.

It's lonely. It's confusing. And it's painful.

When the retreat was over, it was clear that I hit a nerve. Pastors could relate. Many had experienced exile, or they were currently in exile. It was comforting for them to know they were not alone and what they experienced was not unique to them. God had not abandoned them.

In fact, they learned that all God's people are people of exile in one way or another: at one time or another. Hearing my words normalized their experience and showed them a way to return from exile.

Exile is Everyone's Story
After the retreat I decided to expand the teaching into a book: a forty-day spiritual journey for hurting pastors called, *Out of Exile.*

But I knew that pastors weren't the only ones who experienced exile. Everyone experiences a devastating loss that leaves him or her in exile:
> the loss of a loved one…
> the loss of a career…
> the loss of health…
> the loss of financial security…
> the loss of a relationship…
> the loss of reputation.

We all need to learn how to process and grieve our losses so we can reclaim our lives and move on. For this reason, I rewrote *Out of Exile* for the general public and gave it a new name. This is the book you are holding now.

Exile Can Be the Beginning of Something Great
When people first come to know God personally they often think their lives will be safe and full of purpose. That's what well-intentioned believers often promise them. So they are shocked to learn that God might allow them to wander for a season in their own personal exile.

Return from Exile

For example, if you know the Bible, you might recall how Moses lived in a personal exile. After killing an Egyptian to rescue a fellow Hebrew, he lived for forty years tending sheep in the desert. He went from the glory of Pharaoh's palace to the ignobility and isolation of the Sinai wilderness. That was his exile.

But Moses' story shows us that exile is not the end but a new beginning. Exile can be a transition that opens a door from one season of life to the next. I'm sure Moses was disillusioned with the turn of events that took his life so radically off track. After a few decades in the desert he probably resigned himself to finish his days as a lonely shepherd.

But God had other plans.

God used Moses to rescue the Israelites from their slavery and exile in Egypt. His personal exile wasn't the waste of time he thought it was. Exile prepared Moses to be the deliverer of his people.

In the same way, I hope you will learn that whatever trial you have gone through is not the end of your story. You are not finished. You are not a washout. Exile is merely a rite of passage: an intensive character-building workshop preparing you for a richer, fuller life...if you let it.

A 40-Day Journey to Reclaim Your Life
My goal is to help you reclaim your life. I don't want you wandering aimlessly for years, never experiencing the adventures and achievements that God has planned for you. I don't want you giving up on your story because of a setback.

Many people choose to ignore their pain hoping it will eventually go away.

It won't.

The pain will just get buried, and the hurt will remain. Left untended, the pain will grow and eventually impact every area of your life and the people you love as well. It's much better to deal with your losses now than wait until your life slowly unravels.

In the coming pages, I will look at the losses we all face, how the losses create a feeling of "exile," and then how to return from exile. This book is set up as a forty-day devotional: short essays followed by questions to help you move through your time of loss to a place of restoration.

Permission to Grieve
As I look back on the retreat that started this book, I love the conversations it sparked. By introducing the terminology of "exile," it gave people permission to finally talk about their losses. They had a new language to discuss feelings that they hadn't been able to put into words. Talking opened the door that allowed the grief process to begin.

You see, grief is much more than feeling sad. It's a process that moves you to a place of accepting your loss so you can restart your life.

I hope you will find similar benefits as you work your way through this forty-day journey. Process what you learn with your husband or wife, children, counselor, significant other, and friends.

Return from Exile

Don't rush through this book. I know it's tempting. It's a short book that you can read in a day. Take your time. Reflect. Use the forty days to let it sink in. Let it peel back the layers of hurt and confusion that have accumulated since your loss.

Finally, be sure to finish the forty-day journey. It's in the latter pages where I give you concrete steps to make your comeback. Don't quit reading without getting the road map out!

As we begin this journey together, I want to invite God's Spirit to bring healing and wisdom.

Father, you know the hurt my reader carries. You know the journey they are on; the exile they are in. Please use this journey to help them process their loss and grief and start over. Help them to find their way back to the life you've always wanted for them. I invite your Spirit to comfort and guide them along the way. Amen.

F. Remy Diederich, November 2016

How Did I Get Here?

*I'll never forget the sense of "otherness"
I felt during that time.*

As I said in the introduction, exile is how you feel when life throws you a curveball and you end up in a place you never imagined you'd be. You look around and ask yourself: *How on earth did I get here?*

I've gone through my share of exiles. Thankfully, I've come out the other side. But what I learned through the years is that God used my exiles to shape me and prepare me for the life I'm enjoying now. Without my times of exile I would be a much different person. Exile changed me. It deepened me. It broadened me, enabling me to relate to many more people than in my pre-exile days. I want you to be able to say the same thing.

I know I will face more exiles in my future. Exiles are a

part of life. But I am better prepared to meet the challenge of exile after learning the lessons I will share with you here.

My Five Exiles and What Caused Them

To start our journey, I want to give you some context for how I came to learn my lessons in loss. I won't tell my whole story, but I want to briefly outline five causes of the exiles I've gone through. My exiles have a lot to do with my faith and church experience. Maybe you can relate. Maybe you can't. If not, look more to the root *cause* of the exile rather than the specific *experience*.

Scandal

I came to faith at the age of nineteen in a large, upbeat, charismatic church in the 70's. Their success got the best of them. It fell apart after the pastor was exposed in an affair. A church of over 2000 people scattered to the four winds. It doesn't even exist today.

The church had no idea how to handle the pastor's failure. Factions polarized over whether to restore the pastor or throw him out. It was pure chaos. Up until that time, my faith was black and white. I had it all mapped out. I was in the perfect church, but the scandal turned my world upside down. I didn't know what to think. What was once black and white, turned to grey.

Control

Looking for some sanity, I attended a small church that got started out of the large church. I was convinced a small church was the answer to the chaos that I experienced in the large church. At the small church I knew the pastor personally. We were friends. Neighbors. I trusted him. He mentored me to learn a trade to help support me in ministry. He invited me to work part-time for the church, giving me my first chance at "professional" ministry. It was great. I knew everyone in the church. It was a close-knit family. Faith made sense again.

But over time my friend and pastor became increasingly paranoid and controlling. I anguished over what to do. I tried to talk to him, but he didn't see what I was saying. Finally, after receiving two "visions" of warning, he told the congregation that if they left the church something bad would happen to them.

This was too much. I confronted him about his visions, paranoia, and the negative approach he had taken. His response was that I could agree with him or leave. Hurt and disillusioned, I left.

Isolation
When my wife and I left the church, we were cut off from our closest friends. We didn't want to cause them problems with the pastor, or incite them to take up our offense, so we kept our distance. The loss of our community was intense. One day I played some worship music we used to sing in church. I was overcome with a deep sense of grief. I had lost something I couldn't get back.

Then something strange happened inside of us: church suddenly became shallow and cliché. As much as I believed in church, nothing about it felt right. Every few weeks we would try another church to see if we had "gotten over it." But it was always the same.

It was the oddest feeling: like strangers in a strange land

where everyone spoke a different language. I'll never forget the sense of "otherness" I felt during that time. I wondered if I could ever join a church again or be in ministry. I longed for the close ties I once had with my fellow believers. Instead, I was totally alone.

Dysfunction

Not knowing what to do with our new condition, my wife and I gave up on church and moved into an intentional community with two other families. We were confident we could love each other, love Jesus, and live out our faith with so few people involved. How could anything go wrong with such like-minded people in such an idyllic place (a farm in Wisconsin)? You would be amazed how much can go wrong. We disbanded after seven years of agonizing through the intensity of our dysfunctional relationships.

Repression

Toward the end of our farm experience I realized that giving up on church was not the answer. We left the farm and reentered church life where I served as an associate pastor in a somewhat traditional/conservative church. At the time I accepted the position, I didn't realize I was wired to be a lead pastor.

The church was fine, but serving as an associate when I had a heart to lead proved to be very frustrating, and yet another exile. I was confused about what God wanted me to do. I felt called to ministry, but serving as an associate pastor in a conservative church was boring. I felt boxed in. My poor wife had to listen to me lament my dissatisfaction week after week.

I hope these few snapshots from my life help you understand what can cause an exile in your life. Now it's time for you to reflect on your life.

What about you?
- *Can you relate to any of these five causes of exile? Think of examples of each cause listed above.*

- *What are the snapshots from your life that led you into exile?*

- *Can you think of other causes of exile, other than the ones I mentioned?*

DAY TWO

The Six D's of Exile

I was afraid the few good experiences I had were gone forever...

In Day One, I mentioned the causes of my exile. Now I want to give you six words that describe how I felt in exile:

Displaced
Exile feels like being ripped from the safety of your home: uprooted and cast out. You are so far from the familiar that there is nothing to comfort you. It's like waking up to find yourself in another country and realizing that you will never see your home again. My journey led me farther and farther away from where I wanted to be. My initial positive experiences with church seemed to drift farther and farther out of my

grasp.

Disconnected
Once displaced, I was alone. No peers. No family. No tribe. No one who spoke my "language," that is, no one identified with my experience. I thought my experience was unique. It reminds me of Tim Allen's story (the comedian) that I related in my second book (STUCK). In describing his childhood, Tim said that when his father died no one seemed to understand his pain. It was like he was in a boat adrift, all alone.

Disoriented
Disorientation naturally follows from being displaced and disconnected. Nothing is familiar. Life is unsettled because you have no markers to help you get your bearings. You don't know what to do, where to go, or how to think.

Everything is new. You are "born again," only it's not a positive spiritual experience. It means starting over with no maps, or clues, or guideposts. This was especially true for me when I first left the large church. It was the only church I had known up to that point. Coming to faith helped me "find myself," but losing the church made me question everything again.

Disillusioned
Church left me confused for many years. Biblically, I was a believer and understood I was a part of God's Church: his family. But experientially, I was an orphan and that didn't make any sense to me. I asked the same question that everyone asks in exile: *Why would God allow this to happen?*

I had been told my church was "right." It was a New Testament church, just like in the Bible. We had an inside track. We saw things other believers didn't see. Not only did that church fail, but every other expression of church I tried, whether small church or community, failed as well. I was desperate to find a model that worked, but feared there were no answers out there.

Depressed
The lie of loss is: *life will never be good again*. That's how I felt about church and ministry. I was afraid the few good experiences I had were gone forever and I would never enter a true move of God again. It put a cloud over my entire life. I didn't know how to live out my calling without the church.

Full of Doubt
A big part of my exile experience at the traditional church, where I came back into ministry, was the lack of people who saw what I saw. My ideas were continually shot down and told they would never work. (It wasn't until much later, when we started Cedarbrook Church, that we were able to implement these ideas and found they actually did work.)

This happens to young innovators all the time. Their ideas are seen as foolish, or threatening, and it causes them to question their thinking. That's what happened to me. The experience filled me with doubt. I wondered if people were right. Maybe I didn't know what I was talking about. It made me want to quit many times. Thankfully, God sent people my way to encourage me (more on that later) so I didn't give up.

What about you?
- *Can you relate to these feelings? Which ones? How so?*

- *My losses were centered around my church experience. Where do your losses come from?*

- *What are some other words that describe how your exile experience made you feel? (They don't have to start with "D"!)*

DAY THREE

Five Reasons for Ending Up in Exile

*It helps to know what landed you in exile.
It's not always your fault.*

People often think that sin is the only cause for ending up in exile. But that is just one reason. I can think of five reasons why people might end up in exile:

Unbelief
The Bible tells the story of how God's people failed to enter the Promised Land. They failed because they doubted God's ability to help them. As a result, God let them remain in the wilderness, their exile, for forty years until that generation died out. They chose to stay in a barren desert rather than take the risk God called them to take.

Sometimes doubt strands us in a place we never wanted to be. Maybe that's happened to you; you knew the right thing to do, but you refused to follow through out of fear. Now you are in no-man's-land: an exile you created by your own doing.

When I lived on our farm I felt God tell me that it was time to move. I was convinced of it, but then I doubted. I thought there might be a way to make things work. After all, we had invested so much emotionally and financially. How could I just walk away?

Six months later I was desperate in prayer. Problems continued to mount and so I asked God what he wanted me to do. More clearly than ever I sensed God saying: *I already told you what to do.* I immediately remembered my previous sense that God wanted us to move. Doubt had frozen me in place and almost robbed us of what God was calling us to do. My wife and I immediately set plans in motion to move off the farm.

Sin and Rebellion
The Bible tells the story of how God's people entered and lived in the Promised Land for many years. But they lost the right to live there by worshipping false gods. The people did this whenever the competing religion promised something they didn't believe God could deliver like: a good harvest, fertility, financial blessing, revenge, etc.

God spoke through the prophet Ezekiel saying:
>...their children refused to obey me. They did not follow my rules. They were not careful to keep my laws...They misused my Sabbaths. So I said I would pour out all of my burning anger on them

> in the desert...I also raised my hand and took an oath in the desert. I told my people I would scatter them among the nations. I would send them to other countries. They had not obeyed my laws. They had turned their backs on my rules. Ezekiel 20:21,23,24, NIRV.

God scattered his people in exile due to their disobedience. It lasted seventy years.

Maybe you've disobeyed as well. Maybe you've sought to please yourself rather than pleasing God. Your worship shifted from God to cheap substitutes, vices of pleasure that became the new center of your life and devotion. If so, God could send you into exile to get your attention. It's his way of giving you a "time-out" to rethink your priorities in life.

Bad Choices
Bad choices aren't about unbelief or rebellion. You just made some decisions that set you back and put you in a season of exile. Maybe you made bad financial choices that got you in trouble. Maybe you said things that got you in hot water and put your job, or marriage, in jeopardy. Or maybe you allowed yourself to get too busy and the stress of it caused you to burn out or lose connection to your family. Exile can simply be the natural consequence that flows from bad choices.

Bad Luck
Some people end up in exile through no fault of their own. Sometimes bad things just happen for no reason. Tragedy, of all kind, falls into this category: sickness, death, betrayal, a bad economy, crime. I've seen many people lose a loved one unexpectedly and it

threw them into a lifelong exile, never able to regain their bearings. You see, everything doesn't happen for a reason. That's what makes it a tragedy. Tragedies don't make sense. But thankfully God can make good come even out of tragedy.

God's Call
Sometimes God calls us into exile. It's not for any of the reasons above. It's just that God's will can't be accomplished in any other way than through suffering. God didn't spare Jesus from suffering. Jesus' suffering and crucifixion were the ultimate exile.

Maybe God has called you to a season of suffering. For example, maybe you've been called to help someone go through a hard season, like, recover from an addiction. Someone has to do it. You are the one. It's uphill all the way. God's not punishing you. He's using you to bring new life to this person. But it feels like an exile to you.

I mention these five reasons for exile because it helps to know what landed you in exile. When you know what got you into exile, it's easier to find your way out.

What about you?
- *Which of the fives reasons listed above landed you in exile?*

Return from Exile

- *Are there reasons not listed here?*

- *How might knowing the cause help you find the way out?*

Day Four

Laid Bare

God uses exile to expose your true heart...he tears down everything false in you to expose your foundation.

I'm amazed and saddened to see how many people wander in the wilderness for years, wondering what happened to them, having no idea how to get their lives back. Some of them have wandered for decades. Maybe you are one of them.

If you are in exile today, I want to help you find your way out. But to find the way out requires letting exile do its full work in you. Let me explain what I mean by relating a story from the Bible.

After the Israelites disobeyed God for hundreds of years, and after multiple warnings, God allowed the

Return from Exile

Babylonian army to overthrow the Jews living in Jerusalem (586 B.C.). Many people were killed, and many were taken captive to live in Babylon in exile. God spoke to his prophet Ezekiel saying:
> ...son of man, prepare for yourself baggage for exile and go into exile (*galah*)... Ezekiel 12:3, NASB.

The Hebrew word for "go into exile" is "galah." But "galah" also means to "expose, lay bare, uncover, reveal, be stripped."

Here's another verse using "galah," but the word is translated "laid bare:"
> I will tear down the wall you have covered with whitewash and will level it to the ground so that its foundation will be **laid bare** *(galah)*. Ezekiel 13:14, NASB. Emphasis mine.

This means that exile isn't just a *physical* experience. Exile is also a metaphor for what God wants to do *inside* of you. He uses exile to expose your true heart. He "lays you bare," very much like this verse relates: he tears down everything false in you to expose your foundation.

God allows hard times to reveal who you really are. He's not out to shame you or punish you. He wants to purify you by bringing your impurities to the surface and removing them.

Exile reveals your dark side. It has the unique ability to reveal things hidden deep within you that can't be found in good times. In order to move on from exile it requires that you embrace the exile and let God do his full work in you. The more you resist it the longer you stay in exile.

Think of it as spiritual surgery. The best thing you can do is lie still and let the surgeon do her work. Only then can the surgery be complete and you are allowed to move to the recovery room.

What about you?
- *What has exile revealed in your heart?*

- *How well have you done at "lying still" for God to do his work?*

- *What do you think "lying still" entails?*

- *What are some steps you might take after seeing what's in your heart?*

Day Five

Exile is Everywhere

It seems exile is a rite of passage for biblical greatness, yet we dread it like The Plague.

You will be glad to know you are not the only one who has experienced exile. The Bible is full of exile stories.

Adam and Eve were exiled from the Garden of Eden. We've been trying to get back to the Garden ever since. You could say that the entire human race is in exile for that reason.

The Flood was a time of exile for *Noah* as was the new life after the flood. He was cut off from everything he knew and had to struggle through being displaced.

Abraham was in exile in Canaan. Day Six will explore

this more. *Hagar* was exiled from the presence of Abraham and Sarah.

Jacob lived in exile under Laban's rule waiting to receive Rebecca as his wife.

Joseph was in exile in the well and in prison, while *Moses* was in exile many times: in the basket at birth, in the palace growing up, in the wilderness after killing a man, in the Sinai Wilderness, and in his lonely place of leadership.

The *Ark of the Covenant* (God's presence) was in exile when the Israelites took it into battle and the Philistines captured it.

David was in exile as he ran from King Saul and when he allowed his son Absalom to take the kingdom.

Jonathan's son, *Mephibosheth*, was in exile as he sat in the desert for twenty years, unable to use his legs.

Jonah was in exile in the belly of the whale and in Ninevah.

God's people were in exile in Egypt, Assyria, and Babylon.

Mary was in exile as she faced the isolation of being pregnant out of wedlock, even though she knew deep down what God was doing with her.

Jesus was in exile when Satan tempted him, when no one understood him, as he prayed in Gethsemane, as he stood before his accusers, and as he hung on the cross.

Return from Exile

Paul was in exile from the Jews (once his greatest supporters) as well as when he endured his "thorn in the flesh."

And *John* wrote his revelation in exile on the island of Patmos.

It's a wonder why we are so ignorant of exile, and God's purpose for it, when exile is so prevalent in the Bible. How can we be so blind? It seems exile is a rite of passage for biblical greatness, yet we dread it like The Plague.

If we fully understood how God uses exile to benefit us, we would stand in line all night to get into this special "club," or pay a Harvard tuition to gain the wisdom it contains.

But the good news is: we don't have to stand in line, or pay tuition for this education, do we? We all get a free scholarship; it's called "life." We just need to glean the wisdom from it that God has for us.

Why do we think exile is just for ancient times? If God used it then to prove his people, why wouldn't he use it now? He absolutely does.

We can fight against it, or we can embrace it as the gift it is.

What about you?
- *Can you think of other exiles in the Bible?*

- *What has kept you from seeing the value of exile in your life?*

Day Six

I Didn't See This Coming

When there's a famine in the land, you doubt your call, or you doubt God's goodness, or both.

Today I want to look at one exile story in particular: Abraham's (his name was originally Abram). Anyone who is called of God can relate to his story:

> The LORD had said to Abram, "Go from your country, your people and your father's household to the land I will show you. "I will make you into a great nation, and I will bless you; I will make your name great, and you will be a blessing. I will bless those who bless you, and whoever curses you I will curse; and all peoples on earth will be blessed through you." So Abram went, as the LORD had told him; and Lot went with him. Abram was seventy-five years old

when he set out from Harran. He took his wife Sarai, his nephew Lot, all the possessions they had accumulated and the people they had acquired in Harran, and they set out for the land of Canaan, and they arrived there. **Genesis 12:1-5**

As you read this story and reflect on how God has called you, what stands out? When I read Abram's story and compared it to God's calling on my life, I didn't think much of leaving "Haran." Haran symbolizes everything that is familiar. It represents our comfort zone. I was so excited to follow God that I wasn't concerned about that.

I also didn't think much about "being seventy-five." Being seventy-five represents our limitations in life. I was convinced that I could do anything because Jesus lived inside of me.

And I didn't think much about the "Lots" in my life (unhealthy people) who would go with me. I was naïve enough to believe that every Christian is a good person.

No, I didn't think at all about the down side of following Jesus. I focused on verse two: *I will make you into a great nation and I will bless you; I will make your name great, and you will be a blessing.* In other words, I focused on the good things that would come from knowing God, not the losses that might come my way.

I bet that's what Abram heard too. How about you? I'm sure Abram was convinced Canaan would be amazing. Sarah probably wasn't so sure, but Abram was confident she'd come around once she saw what a great place it was.

Return from Exile

In Canaan, Abram was going to establish God's kingdom! In Canaan, he was going to be the MAN. God's man. He was going to call the shots and make things happen in a way he never could as long as he was under his dad's oversight back in Haran.

Canaan was definitely the land of promise! Abram couldn't get there fast enough.

Did you respond to God's call that way, that is, all you saw was the glory – the possibilities?

But what did Abram find in Canaan?
> At that time the Canaanites were in the land. Genesis 12:6

Wait a minute. Canaanites? (Canaanites worshipped their gods by sacrificing their children to them.) *God never said anything about Canaanites.* Maybe that's how you responded to the first problem that came your way after deciding to follow Jesus: *God never told me I'd lose my job, or have a dry season in my marriage, or one of my kids would go astray, or my health would fail! What's the deal?*

But that's not all Abram had to deal with. There's more. Or, I should say, less:
> Now there was a famine in the land... Genesis 12:10

A famine? If God called me, how could there be a famine? I thought God would take care of my needs. I didn't think I'd have to face suffering.

And then come the doubts: *Maybe God's not real, or at*

least not personal like I thought he was. Maybe he doesn't care. Maybe I can't count on him. Maybe prayer is useless. When there's a famine in the land, you doubt God is personal, or you doubt God's goodness, or both.

There are many losses associated with following after God. That's not bad. Some things need to be lost. But it's important to understand that losses are part of your spiritual journey. Salvation doesn't mean being saved from your problems. It means that God walks with you *through* your problems.

Too often we suffer loss but never deal with it. We put our heads down, keep working, and "trust the Lord" that it will all work out. What we don't realize is that, by ignoring our losses, we are actually setting ourselves up for greater exile later on…an exile from which we may never return.

What about you?
- *What were some of your expectations in life that haven't been met? Be honest.*

- *What are some losses you've encountered that you never saw coming?*

- *How have these losses affected you and your relationship with God...really?*

Day Seven

Embracing Your Dark Side

We are all "Abram" before God transforms us into "Abraham."

Let's keep looking at Abram's early days. I'm speculating that Abram was excited at God's call to move to Canaan. He was full of hope with visions of changing the world for God. But when he got to Canaan he was met with two unexpected companions: Canaanites and famine. He didn't see them coming.

It shouldn't surprise us that as soon as Abram arrived in Canaan, he quickly felt compelled to leave.

> Abram went down to Egypt to live there for a while because the famine was severe. Genesis 12:10

Return from Exile

I wonder if you've ever done that...left a place soon after you got there...maybe a job, or even a marriage? The "famine" was too great. You didn't know what you had bargained for. You thought you heard from God, but then everything was so foreign: so hard. You became disillusioned and looked for a way out. Sometimes it's easier to just leave and start over (at least, that's what we think).

I have a young friend, Sam, who joined a church out of seminary. The church had an aging pastor headed for retirement, and they were looking to bring in some fresh blood to attract younger families. The pastor was eager to share his leadership and the governing board promised to support new ideas, so Sam took the job with visions of a smooth transition.

Can you guess what happened? Everyone sang a different song once Sam was on staff. His ideas were too controversial to the board, and the pastor didn't want to give up control. In fact, he thought he had a few more years left in him.

Sam was crushed and wondered if he missed God's will for his life by taking this position. He anguished over what to do for a number of months and eventually left, wondering what just happened.

That's what Abram did. He left Canaan. But things went from bad to worse. When he got to Egypt he encountered the powerful Pharaoh. He was afraid Pharaoh would kill him, and take his wife, so he told his wife:
> Say you are my sister, so that I will be treated well for your sake and my life will be spared

F. Remy Diederich

because of you. Genesis 12:13

This is a nice way to say, *Please prostitute yourself to save my butt.* Pharaoh was always looking to add another beautiful woman to his harem, and that's what he did when he saw Sarah.

Abram did two things he probably never thought he'd do: lie and sell out his wife. How could this happen? What could drive him to do these things? *Exile.*

Exile puts you to the test and reveals your dark side. That's one of the main reasons we hate it so much. Not only do we hate the "Canaanites" and the "famine," we hate seeing the ugly way we respond to the stress and temptations in exile.

We like to think we are better than that; we are above that. This is where many people turn to denial to salve their pain. They don't want to see the person they really are. But the bold and the brave embrace their dark side and invite God to do his work in them.

Abram's story was given by God to help everyone called by God. We are all "Abram" before God transforms us into "Abraham". The word "Abram" means "father," and the word "Abraham" means "father of many people." Exile is what God used to transform Abram from merely a father, to a *father of many*.

I'm sure Abraham was embarrassed at his behavior and full of regret. Yet, God still used him to become the father of faith. If God can transform Abraham's failure, he can transform yours too. God wants to use your exile to take your life to an entirely new level. Can you believe that?

What about you?
- *Have you ever left a job, relationship, etc. that you felt called to, but couldn't handle it? What were the losses that caused you to leave? Were there more losses that followed your leaving?*

- *How have your exiles exposed your dark side? What specifically was revealed?*

- *How did you handle that? Did you face your dark side, run from it, or cover it up?*

- *How might God use your exile (your loss) to take your life to an entirely new level?*

Day Eight

Eight Types of Exile

There is no quick fix to exile. It's like a seed in the ground. It needs to suffer many days in the dark before something is birthed, grows, and bears fruit.

Today is the last day of defining exile. In days to come, I'll look at what we learn in exile and then, ultimately, how to return from exile. Be patient. I know you want to find the way out of your exile. But there is no quick fix. It's like a seed in the ground. It needs to suffer many days in the dark before something is birthed, grows, and bears fruit.

We typically think of exile as when people are forced to leave their country. But as I said before, living in exile isn't just about being displaced. There are many aspects to exile. Earlier I spoke about five specific causes of exile that I have experienced. Today I want to explore eight general types of exile.

Emotional Exile

As you know, there's a dark side to our emotions. It includes problems like depression, posttraumatic stress (PTSD), anxiety, panic attacks, bipolar disorder, and many others. One commenter to my blog said he struggled for years with the "exile" of addiction until he was diagnosed as bi-polar. That changed his life. He was put on medication that delivered him from his addiction. But until that happened, his life was a barren wilderness.

Spiritual Exile

Many people struggle seeking and finding God. For some it's natural. For others, God is confusing and covered in clouds. Some have called their separation from God their "dark night of the soul." Bad church experiences, or bad encounters with "spiritual" people, can add to this confusion/disillusionment. You are left wondering if there even is a God.

Relational Exile

God created us for relationships. When our relationships break down, or never happen to begin with, the disconnection can consume us. Divorce, estrangement from children/parents, death of a loved one, co-worker tension, singleness, and bad marriages are just a few of the relational exiles we experience.

Financial Exile

Nothing consumes us quicker than the loss of income. It immediately grabs our attention and insists on controlling every waking thought. You can't rest when you are worrying how you will pay your bills.

Career Exile

Looking for work can feel like exile, especially if it goes on for an extended period of time. The continual flow of rejection makes you wonder if you fit in this world. It eats away at your sense of identity.

It's especially hard when you thought your job was a call from God. If you can't find work, what does that say about your calling? Were you wrong? What does it say about God? Did he trick you? Let you down? If you accept a job in a different field are you letting God down? Or, if you finally find a job and it turns out to be a bad match (like for my friend Sam) is it right to leave and start over? These are tough questions that can bounce around your brain unanswered for months, even years.

Physical Exile

We take our health for granted until it leaves us. Wrestling with chronic pain, burnout, injuries, the inability to have children, or a terminal disease are just a few examples of problems that can lead to a sense of exile.

I've always been healthy but over the last year I've had a few physical struggles (phantom fatigue and sports injuries). I'm surprised how much it has affected me emotionally. My inability to do what I want to do, at the level I want to do it, has proven to be a big loss for me. When I drive by a runner, a sadness often falls over me, knowing that I'm not able to enjoy a run like I have in the past.

Season of Life Exile
Transitions between seasons of life might seem minor, but they often surprise us and leave us in exile. The time between college and marriage and/or career, marriage, childbirth, the empty nest, retirement, and old age can all present exile experiences. Each transition is like starting from zero. You've never been in this place before. You haven't taken any classes on how to handle it, and there is no one to guide you through it.

Success Exile
This might not be obvious, but success can lead to a transition in life you weren't prepared for. I've experienced some ministry success that I didn't anticipate. When I achieved results that went beyond what I ever imagined, I was disoriented for a number of months and even depressed. I achieved what I wanted and didn't know what to do next. I lost my purpose for a season before getting refocused on the next phase of my life.

The experience of exile is everywhere, once we know what it looks like. It's helpful to be aware of it so you can deal with it appropriately.

What about you?
- *How many types of exile impact you?* Rank them in order of impact on you.

- *What do you think the compounding impact of these exiles has on your life?*

- *Can you think of other types of exile?*

- If you are feeling sad right now, don't suppress it. Explore it. Ask God to show you what's behind the sadness.

Day Nine

Experiencing Loss

Most of us are ill prepared for loss...
Are we that optimistic or that naïve?

Today I want to look a little deeper at what sends us into exile in the first place. Of course, outright sin is the fast track to exile. I mentioned this earlier. Moral failure can sideline us for years. Most people can connect the dots to this familiar path to exile. But I want to focus on the more subtle causes of exile.

Put simply, what sends you into exile is *a sense of loss*. When your experience in life falls short of what you expected would happen, the difference between the two is a loss. Remember what happened to Abraham? He expected glory. He experienced famine. That was a loss.

F. Remy Diederich

EXPECTATION

LOSS

EXPERIENCE

Most of us are ill prepared for loss. I'm not sure why that is. Are we that optimistic, or that naïve? We see loss all around us. But we rarely think it will happen to us. When it does, we are often devastated and disillusioned as if the thought never occurred to us that something bad could ever happen. The surprise of loss compounds our exile experience.

Loss produces a variety of uncomfortable emotions. The big three are:
- **Anger**: you are mad that your expectation wasn't met and mad at whomever you think is responsible.
- **Sadness**: you mourn the loss of what you expected to have forever.
- **Fear**: you are afraid that you will never achieve your expectation: that loss will be a way of life from now on.

These emotions are normal. In fact, these emotions are good. If you didn't have an emotional response to loss, there would be something wrong with you. We have a word for people who don't show normal emotions: *sociopath*. So be glad you have emotions. God gave you emotions to fully experience life and move you to action.

But, be careful; you don't want to get stuck in your emotions. You want to *move through* your emotions to a better place. It's easy to stuff your emotions as a "quick-fix" to their discomfort. It's also easy to vent them thinking that's how you get release. Instead, why not explore your emotions to learn what's going on inside your head and heart?

Your emotions give you a clue to wrong - even toxic - thinking that might be hiding deep inside you. They are your "Geiger counter" to tell you that something is wrong. When your emotions fire, ask God to use them to pinpoint trouble spots that require healing.

What about you?
- *What are some emotions you've experienced from loss?*

- *How do you handle your emotions? Do you stuff them or vent them? What's been the outcome from that behavior?*

- *What have you learned about yourself and God from your emotions?*

Day Ten

Denying Your Loss

For some, sin leads them into exile.
For others, exile is what leads them to sin.

Anger, fear, and sadness operate like a *Band of Brothers*. It's almost impossible to have one without the other. That's why it's important that you learn to identify them in your life and have a plan to deal with each one.

Unfortunately, the quick solution to these emotions is denial. *Feel bad?* No problem. Just immerse yourself in behavior that drowns out the noise from your loss. Numb yourself with your favorite tonic.

We've all been there. Denial looks different to everybody. It can be socially acceptable behavior like: working too much, or over-indulging in hobbies, or exercise, or "social" drinking. But for too many, their response to loss goes way beyond socially acceptable. Their loss can bring such strong disillusionment that people feel justified in throwing off any inhibitions they once had. They dive headlong into alcohol and drug abuse, pornography, an affair, misuse of funds, or any behavior that helps them escape the pain of their loss.

Their misguided thinking says: *If life doesn't make sense, then why bother trying to keep the rules?* That's why we are often shocked to learn about the secret lifestyles of people who were once known for their integrity and moral influence. For some, sin leads them into exile. For others, exile is what leads them to sin.

The most common form of denial is to simply minimize your loss. Christians do this effortlessly because they have Bible based clichés ready to do the job. What do we say when confronted with loss? *I'm just trusting the Lord. The Lord gives and he takes away.* Insert your favorite Bible cliché here.

The problem with clichés isn't that they are untrue. The problem is they shutdown the thinking and grief process. You should absolutely trust in the Lord. He *will* bring you through your loss. BUT, it still hurts. It's still a loss. You can't just act like nothing happened and move on with your life, "trusting the Lord."

Grief requires that you acknowledge your loss, admit the impact it had on you, give yourself permission to feel terrible about it for a season, and resolve the issues that come from the loss. THEN you can move on, but not before. Part of "trusting the Lord," is trusting him to see you through the grieving process to full acceptance of your loss.

This grieving process I just described isn't sin, like some Christians think it is. They would say that if you reflect on your loss, you aren't trusting God. You are turning to human psychology. But God made us *human*. Humans hurt. We feel pain. We get sad. And that's okay. It's necessary.

But church people don't always give themselves permission to be human. They think they have to be above human emotion and so they spiritualize their loss by trivializing it. What they don't realize is that when they minimize their loss, it sits in their heart rotting for years, souring them on life. It occasionally sends out shock waves of anger and depression, but since the loss is buried so deep, they never make the connection. They blame their feelings on current irritations, when in reality; the emotions are linked to a past loss.

If you haven't already started, it's time to ask yourself what your losses are, and then what emotions you have in response to the losses. Once you can answer these questions, it would be great for you to share your losses with God first, and then your spouse, friend, or counselor. This is necessary before you can start your return from exile.

What about you?
- *What are some ways you have denied your losses?*

- *What are some clichés you use to minimize loss?*

- *What keeps you from giving yourself permission to face your losses?*

- *Do you think it is a sin to allow yourself to feel the pain of loss and grieve it? If so, why?*

Day Eleven

Journaling Your Exile

The evidence is mounting that the act of writing about traumatic experience ... can produce measurable changes in physical and mental health.
James Pennebaker

In Day Ten, I talked about denial and how we often minimize our losses by over spiritualizing them. But a woman told me that she often had the opposite problem. She had too much emotion. Rather than minimize and deny her losses, she would obsess over them, allowing them to consume her life. She needed to find ways to channel her emotion in positive ways. She said journaling was one positive approach she took.

Brene Brown quotes some research in her book, *Daring Greatly*, that relates to journaling:

In a pioneering study, psychologist and University of Texas professor James Pennebaker and his colleagues studied what happened when trauma survivors— specifically rape and incest survivors— kept their experiences secret. The research team found that the act of not discussing a traumatic event or confiding it to another person could be more damaging than the actual event.

Conversely, when people shared their stories and experiences, their physical health improved, their doctor's visits decreased, and they showed significant decreases in their stress hormones. Since his early work on the effects of secret keeping, Pennebaker has focused much of his research on the healing power of expressive writing.

In his book, Writing to Heal, Pennebaker writes, "Since the mid-1980s an increasing number of studies have focused on the value of expressive writing as a way to bring about healing. The evidence is mounting that the act of writing about traumatic experience for as little as fifteen or twenty minutes a day for three or four days can produce measurable changes in physical and mental health. Emotional writing can also affect people's sleep habits, work efficiency, and how they connect with others." (p. 82)

Brene Brown notes the Alcoholic's Anonymous saying: *you are only as sick as your secrets;* her point being that it's important to process your pain with someone, even if it's yourself through journaling. You need to expose your secrets.

Everyone needs an outlet for their thoughts and emotions without apologizing for them. Once you get your thoughts down on paper it's easier to "own" them, meaning, you can admit how you really feel and begin to deal with your losses honestly and effectively.

Some people don't want to talk or journal about their problems for fear they aren't trusting God. They think they shouldn't need these outlets. All they need is God. Not true! God wants to give us tangible outlets to help us process our problems. It's not a sign of weak faith to want, or need, to share our pain with another person and resolve it. It's a sign of our humanity and our willingness to "dare greatly" (as Brene Brown would say).

What about you?
- *Do you journal? Why or why not? If so, how has it helped you to process loss?*

- *What other ways have you found helpful to share your pain in constructive ways?*

- Consider journaling for a week to see if it offers you any help.

Day Twelve

Secondary Losses

There are two levels of loss: primary and secondary.

People get stuck in exile because of their unresolved anger. They just can't get past what happened to them. But, in sorting out your anger, you should know that there are two levels of loss: *primary* and *secondary*.

Here's a simple example of what I'm talking about. Do you ever lose your car keys? I do. I hope I'm not the only one. It drives me crazy. I get so mad at myself. One time, after fuming about my keys, I stopped and asked myself why that was. I mean, I knew I would find them eventually (maybe in my pocket). They were obviously in the house because the car was in the garage. So, why the anger? What was the big deal?

It dawned on me that my anger came from more than just my primary loss (the keys). It came from all the losses that follow, what I call: *secondary* losses. The secondary loss is the loss that comes as a *result* of losing my keys.

For example: I didn't just lose the keys. I lost time looking for them. Now I'm late. But being late leads to more loss. Because I'm late I lose my sense of calm. When my wife tries to help me, I vent my frustration on her, losing my connection with her. When I finally find my keys, I drive faster, which might end in a speeding ticket. Now I lose money. When I walk into work late I might lose respect. People say...*Remy's late again...I can never count on him.*

You see, it's not just losing my keys that is so upsetting. It's all the other losses that come with the loss of the keys: real or imagined. If I had to assign responsibility for my emotion, I'd say that only 20% of my anger has to do with the lost keys and 80% has to do with the losses *associated* with the loss of my keys.

Now, take that example and apply it to what I've said about the bigger losses in life: loss of a loved one, loss of a job, loss of your marriage, loss of health, loss of the ability to bear children, etc. (the list is endless). Each event, on its own, is painful. But it represents only 20% of the real issue.

Many people never identify the real issue. They see the "car keys." They don't see the "loss of respect." They spend their time lamenting the keys, blaming the keys, blaming their wife who is no help in finding the keys, asking God to give them new keys, etc. They think they are in exile because of the keys. Hardly. The "keys" are not the issue. Helping you regain your "keys" isn't what God is after. He's after something much deeper in you: the secondary losses.

Imagine losing your marriage through divorce. That's painful. But don't over focus on the primary loss (the person). There's more to it than that. There are the secondary losses: the loss of respect from your spouse and his or her friends, the loss of control because you couldn't do anything to stop it, the loss of income that results from the divorce, the loss of "Plan A," that is, the life you've dreamed about, and the loss of identity now that you are no longer a spouse and only a "half-time" parent.

Whether you are able to see the secondary losses or not will determine if you ever make it out of exile. When I understood secondary losses, it became a defining moment in my life. I can now look quickly past the primary loss to ask myself deeper questions like:

- *Why do I need to be respected by those who reject me?*
- *Why did the loss cause me to lose my sense of identity?*
- *Why do I feel so lost?*
- *Why do I need to be in control?*
- *Do I really think God has failed me?*

These are the kinds of questions that lead to deep insight and allow you to return from exile.

What about you?
- You are probably aware of the primary losses in your life. Write them down. *Now, what are the secondary losses associated with each primary loss?*

- *What are some of the questions that plague you because of your secondary losses?*

Day Thirteen

Invalidation

Invalidation is a part of living in this world and it has sent many into exile.

In Day Twelve I talked about secondary losses and how not knowing about them can leave you in exile. Over the next few days I want to talk about four categories of primary loss and the secondary losses that accompany them. Remember, a primary loss is like "losing your car keys," while the secondary loss is how "losing your car keys" affects you emotionally.

The first category of loss is invalidation. To invalidate you is to insult you or put you down. It means to show you disrespect or discredit you, causing you to feel diminished, embarrassed, and even worthless.

Simon Cowell made a name for himself invalidating people on the TV talent show, *American Idol.* His put-downs drew boos and catcalls from the audience. You could often see the contestants visually wilt on stage, wishing they could find a hole to crawl in.

We all have areas of vulnerability that set us up for the mini-Simon Colwell's whom are quick to invalidate us. Bosses are notorious for humiliating their reports. Your best effort might be taken for granted or the credit given to someone else. Worse yet is when they point out a failure in front of your peers.

A friend of mind is notably overweight. He knows it. He's not proud of it. He told me that inevitably someone will make a joke about his weight every day. He smiles on the outside. But on the inside he feels like a failure, unable to lose the weight that others seem to never put on.

Parents are notorious for pointing out what's wrong with their children before noticing what they do right. The classic example is viewing the report card full of "A's" but choosing to wonder aloud why there is a C or B on the report.

Husbands wonder what their stay-at-home wives "do all day." Wives make jokes about their "dumb husbands" in front of their female friends.

School kids call each other cruel names.

Christians dismiss people as "sinners" without taking time to understand their situation.

My personal sense of invalidation is when people ask me what I do for a living. That's a guaranteed conversation stopper! Few people ask follow up questions when I tell them I'm a pastor.

Secondary Losses
Invalidation is the primary loss. What are the secondary losses associated with being invalidated? One is the loss of respect. Everyone wants to be treated with dignity and have their work appreciated. We want to feel valued for who we are and what we do. When that's missing, it hurts.

A second loss is control. You want to stop people from saying hurtful things to you. Or, in my case, I want people to take an interest in how I've invested my life, but I can't make them be interested. Having no control over your life is unsettling.

Invalidation is a part of living in this world and it has sent many into exile.

What about you?
- *What are some ways you experience invalidation?*

- *What are the secondary losses that you struggle with by being invalidated?*

- *Can you think of other secondary losses associated with being invalidated?*

Day Fourteen

Limited Choices

The more choice you have, the more power and control you feel. Take that power away and it hurts.

We looked at the pain of being invalidated. Let's look at another loss: limited choices.

Whenever your choices are limited, that's a loss. For example, if I tell a five-year-old to pick out just *one* candy bar from the rack of one hundred choices, he may lament the "loss" of 99 candy bars more than he celebrates the possession of one. He doesn't like his choices to be limited. It's human nature to focus on what you can't have instead of what you do have.

The more choice you have, the more power and control you feel. Take that power away and it hurts. When your choices are limited it complicates your life. It's like you are in a card game and you only get dealt half a hand. Or, it's like being forced to work with one hand tied behind your back. It puts you at a huge disadvantage, which is maddening.

Sometimes our choices limit other choices. For example, the choice to get married is celebrated. But over time, the couple might feel like they've lost more in the relationship than they've gained. The loss of independence is more than they bargained for and, what started as euphoria, slowly turns into an exile.

I've heard back from a number of people who joined the armed forces who became incensed when they learned they'd be sent into the heat of battle. They didn't join the army to go to war! They joined to see the world, or to get a paycheck. The thought of being forced into battle wasn't a limitation they were willing to face.

If you are in ministry, the minute you chose the ministry, you limited your choices in life, whether you knew it or not. For example, a pastor friend of mine was struggling financially and he realized that, short of getting another job, he didn't have any way to increase his income. Working longer hours or working harder made no impact on his income like it does in some professions. He was stuck financially and he was mad about it.

Secondary Losses
When life limits your choices, as I just described, be careful not to blame the primary loss (getting married, joining the military, entering ministry). Look deeper to the secondary losses. This is where you gain insight.

There are a number of secondary losses related to limited choices. I've mentioned one already: the loss of control. Dallas Willard talks about the importance of a person having the ability to control their lives:

> In creating human beings God made them to rule, to reign, to have dominion in a limited sphere. Only so can they be persons. Any being that has say over nothing at all is no person... They would be reduced to completely passive observers who count for nothing, who make no difference.[2]

Dallas is saying that when you have no control over your life, it's easy to feel diminished as a person. You lose your sense of freedom and independence: your ability *to have dominion in a limited sphere.*

I'll never forget the first time I visited someone in prison. I was struck by their lack of choice. They were led around like a dog on a leash. They weren't mistreated, but they had lost their "dominion in a limited sphere." It was easy to see how someone could lose their sense of dignity. Their exile was more than physical. It was emotional too.

What about you?
- Think through your life. *Where have your choices been limited?* Those are the primary losses. *Now think deeper; what are the emotional losses associated with those limited choices?* Those are the secondary losses.

- *Can you think of other secondary losses that result from limited choices?* Besides control, others might be: respect, freedom, self-image, sense of identity, creativity, progress, etc.

- Bring all of these losses to God. Tell him how you feel. Ask him to speak to you about these losses. *What does God want you to know about these primary and secondary losses?*

Day Fifteen

Personal Trauma

Many of us live with the unrealistic belief that we live in an impervious bubble that protects us 24/7. We think other people are subject to the cruelties of life. Not us.

Let's continue the discussion of primary and secondary losses by looking at personal trauma.

In his book, *A Grace Disguised,* Jerry Sittser tells the story of how three members of his family were taken in one tragic car accident. This is what he said about loss after experiencing his own:

> We live life as if it were a motion picture. Loss turns life into a snapshot. The movement stops; everything freezes. We find ourselves looking at picture albums to remember the motion picture of our lives that once was but can no longer be.

Loss turns life into a snapshot. That's an interesting analogy. Lenore Terr, author of *Too Scared to Cry*, uses another film analogy:

> The memory of trauma is shot with higher intensity light than is ordinary memory. And the film doesn't seem to disintegrate with the usual half-life of ordinary film. Only the best lenses are used, lenses that will pick up every last detail, every line, every wrinkle, and every fleck. There is more detail picked up during traumatic events than one would expect from the naked eye under ordinary circumstances.

That's what happened with Sittser. His life was moving along fine, like a motion picture, until the car crash. Then he was handed a high definition snapshot of loss to always remind him of what once was, but could no longer be. He comments on how anger relates to loss:

> Anger is simply another way of deflecting the pain, holding it off, fighting back at it. But the pain of loss is unrelenting. It stalks and chases until it catches us. It is as persistent as wind on the prairies, as constant as cold in the Antarctic, as erosive as a spring flood.

What a vivid picture of the pain of loss. Maybe that has happened to you: the death of a loved one, the loss of your job or ministry, the end of a marriage, a miscarriage, physical or emotional burn-out, or any kind of life altering setback. Remember: it's not just the loss that sends you into exile. It's the injustice of the *secondary* losses associated with the setback.

Secondary Losses

So what are some of the secondary losses associated with trauma? One of the biggest losses is the sudden realization that life is not safe and predictable; you have no control. You are vulnerable to the whims of nature and the choices other people make.

Many of us live with the unrealistic belief that we live in an impervious bubble that protects us. We think *other* people are subject to the cruelties of life. *Not us.* But when trauma finally strikes, our bubble bursts, and it sends us reeling. Not only is there a loss of a sense of safety and control but often a loss of faith. Why would God let this happen? Maybe you've asked this same question. Exploring these secondary losses will help you return from exile.

What about you?

- *What snapshots are you holding that keep you in emotional exile?*

- *Which emotions have the biggest hold on you: anger, fear, or sadness? Others?*

- *What are the secondary losses you've experienced as a result of trauma?*

- *Do you feel abandoned by God because of past trauma?*

Day Sixteen

Bittersweet

One moment I am overwhelmed with thankfulness, the next filled with disappointment.

When I first posted my thoughts on loss and trauma in a blog series, I received an email from a friend whose son was diagnosed with brain cancer. The boy had a tumor removed successfully, but the following year was a trying time as the family worked their way through both radiation and chemo treatments.

I thought her expression of the pain and joy of this year captured the essence of what it means to be in exile:

> *Life is full of blessings and heartaches. At times I look at my son and feel joy and praise for the progress he has made. Moments later I look at his precious bald head and am filled with the deepest*

sadness I have ever felt, thinking of all he has been through and still must endure.

One moment I feel my plate is full, the next I am begging God to show me my purpose in life. One moment marriage feels deep, right and intimate, the next it feels like more than I have to give. One moment my heart is full of the deepest love for my boys, the next irritation and frustration arise because the mom responsibilities feel too much.

One moment God feels so close with my faith expanding beyond what I ever could have imagined, the next moment fear overwhelms and grips me to the core. One moment I am overwhelmed with thankfulness, the next filled with disappointment.

Persevering this journey is hard. Almost a year later I am left to truly depend on God's promises that he will be strong enough and loving enough to grow me up through this journey and that all things will work for the good for those who love the Lord.

My heart is heavy ...

What about you?
- *Can you relate to the bittersweet nature of her exile?* Take a minute to share which of her words resonate with you the most. Why is that?

Return from Exile

- *Are there other contradictory feelings that you have in your exile?*

DAY SEVENTEEN

Unmet Needs

My wife ...gets a husband that has been run over, then backed over, and then steamrolled.

In my book, STUCK...*how to overcome anger and reclaim your life*, I discuss seven primary losses.[3] The fourth loss I'm relating here is unmet needs. An unmet need is any area of your life where a legitimate need exists, but it goes unmet by God, or those you look to for help.

When I moved off our farm and into ministry, I was so poor, any salary seemed like a fortune to me. So, I was grateful for the salary I was given by the church that hired me. But it wasn't long before I realized that I couldn't live on it.

I told the church leadership about my dilemma and they

seemed concerned, but they never did anything about it. To make ends meet, I started selling my blood plasma. The senior pastor said he felt bad for me and they needed to do something about it. But they didn't, at least at that time. After many months of making requests, I was finally given a livable wage.

I cleaned out my office files the other day and I came across a letter I wrote to the church governing board telling them how frustrated I was that they hadn't done anything about my salary. It hurt to look back and feel the pain of that time. Have you been in a place like that?

Not only do we hurt when our needs aren't met, our family is hurt too. *Our* losses cause *them* losses. Here's how one man put it to me:

> Coming home with heavy burdens has... brought struggles at home. My wife knows the difficulties that come my way each day and at times she gets a husband that has been run over, then backed over, and then steamrolled. Not much left, and perhaps not that enjoyable to be with. Life at home can become trying and my family gets what is left. Not sure how to describe all that was lost at home, but I do know a significant amount of pain and loss has taken place...

Unmet needs go way beyond finances. It might be time off. It might be the lack of friends. It could be a spouse that you aren't connecting with very well. Or it might be a career that is less than stellar. You have no sense of accomplishment.

Secondary Losses

But remember, these are all *primary* losses. There are secondary losses associated with unmet needs. As is often the case, one loss here is control. You can't *make* people meet your needs. It's frustrating. You feel trapped with no ability to alter your situation. You wonder how long it will go on. Will it ever change? Should I communicate my needs *again*? These feelings and questions are where the sense of "exile" kicks in.

Another secondary loss is respect. When your needs are ignored you wonder why people don't care. How can they just look past your obvious need? Are you that insignificant? Is your work valued so little?

Unmet needs can also result in a loss of purpose. You begin to doubt God's calling on your life. If your needs aren't being met, maybe it's because God doesn't want you in that place or that job. You might think he is withholding his blessing to get your attention so you will move on.

When you have unmet needs, it puts you in a holding pattern, waiting for the pieces to come together so you can take your next step. But the waiting game is often longer than you ever imagined.

You may have noticed that two of the most prominent secondary losses are "respect" and "control." When these two ingredients are missing from your life it's easy to slip into a state of exile. This is where faith in God can play such an important role because he can give you what others can't. When no one else respects you, God does. And when you've lost all control, God hasn't. You can trust him with your life.

What about you?

- *With which of the unmet needs mentioned can you most identify?*

- *What are the secondary losses that came with your unmet needs?*

- With all of these losses the natural emotional response is anger, sadness, and often fear. It's these emotions that create the feeling of exile. *With which of these emotions can you identify?*

- *How can God help meet you in your secondary losses?*

Day Eighteen

Traveling Companions

Exile is a place of isolation. Part of the intense pain of exile is a feeling of being cut off: abandoned.

Exile is a place of isolation. Part of the intense pain of exile is feeling cut off: abandoned. You might be *literally* cutoff: separated from friends or loved ones by distance, death, or divorce. Or, you might be *emotionally* cut off through betrayal or rejection.

In my different times of exile, isolation was very real, but God brought companions into my life to comfort and encourage me. Here are three companions God sent my way.

People
I can point to many people throughout my life that

encouraged me to keep going at just the right time; too many to mention here. But I'll mention two couples.

When we lived on our farm, we were not only very poor but our relationships with our co-owners weren't very strong. As a result, we experienced isolation in a way that was new to us. It was doubly painful because our expectation was that our relationships would be *stronger* on the farm, not weaker.

But thankfully we met a family at church who had children with ages mirroring ours. They were at the opposite end of the financial spectrum, but they never let that get in between our friendship. Their willingness to include us in their lives came at the lowest time for us. When they invited us over for a meal in their spacious home, it was a reprieve from our meager life on the farm and we felt God used them to encourage us.

When that family moved, God brought another couple into our lives. In fact, they have become some of our closest friends and ministry supporters to this day. Later on, when we started Cedarbrook Church, God brought several key people to stand with us, letting us know that we weren't alone in our venture. It's so interesting to experience the support of people in these moments because they have no idea how God is using their simple gestures to keep you going one more day.

Books

I've always been a reader. During my exiles different authors brought grace and truth into my world to make sense of what was happening. I will share some quotes from them in the coming days.

The Bible

The Bible went flat to me for several years. That was an "exile" all its own. But during my farm years I opened it again, turning to Genesis 12, and started to read about Abraham. For whatever reason, his story came alive. I saw that Abraham's exile was much like mine. I felt like I came to know him personally and heard God speak to me through his story.

Over time, other stories took on the same kind of meaning for me, whether the stories were of Moses, David, Samson, or Paul, their lives are now beacons of light to me in times of darkness.

My point here is that God doesn't leave you totally alone in exile. He has words of encouragement for you out there some place to help you keep going. So look for them, even in unsuspecting places. Maybe the person you want for a friend isn't the person God wants to use in your life. Look harder. You might be looking right past God's chosen vessel to comfort you.

What about you?
- *What companions has God brought your way in your exile?* Consider thanking them.

- *Who else might God want to use to speak to you? Are you looking past anyone?*

- *Are there people you might seek out for counsel?*

- Consider starting a reading program. Read stories of people who have been used by God. See how God helped them through their difficulties in life to bring them out of exile and into a good place.

Day Nineteen

Lamentation

I felt like an utter failure. It was humiliating...We went there to experience a little bit of heaven, but sometimes life felt more like a living hell.

On Day Eighteen I said God sends companions to us in exile to comfort and encourage us. One of those comforters for me, back in my days on the farm, was the word from Jeremiah the prophet. He wrote a letter of mourning after the destruction of Jerusalem. Because he experienced that devastation firsthand, he understood the depths of loss.

After he reflected on his loss he wrote:
> It is good for a young man to work hard while he is young. He should sit alone and be quiet; the Lord has given him hard work to do.

Return from Exile

Lamentation 3:27,28, NCV.

That got my attention. I was certainly working hard. We had moved from the Twin Cities to a farm in Wisconsin with two other families. It was a utopian dream to create a Christian community, but it didn't work out that way. We ended up working harder than I ever imagined. And at the end of the day we were more in debt than when we started. It was very discouraging.

Jeremiah continues:
> He should bow down to the ground; maybe there is still hope. He should let anyone slap his cheek; he should be filled with humility. Lamentations 3:29,30, NCV.

That's how I felt, like life was slapping me around. Nothing I did succeeded. Just about everything in my life struggled: my marriage, my faith, my finances, my parenting, etc. Things broke that I couldn't fix. I'd just stand and stare at what I broke, totally powerless to fix it. Animals died from my mistakes. I can't tell you how devastating that was.

I felt like an utter failure. It was humiliating. I didn't understand why our plans for community failed. We thought we heard from God. We went there to experience a little bit of heaven, but sometimes life felt more like a living hell.

My guess is, you know exactly what I mean. You too feel slapped around and you wonder if anything good can come from it. Can things get any worse?

Jeremiah's words might sound depressing, but they

really helped me understand what God might be doing at that time in my life. I felt like God was using my experience to break me of my pride; but if I worked through it, I'd come out on the other side a better person, better able to do God's will.

You see, before the farm, I was overconfident. I didn't know that, but I was. I thought that if I just worked hard enough and smart enough, and with God's help, I could accomplish anything. I could even be profitable farming! That's how delusional I was! The farm experience revealed my overconfidence. God showed me he wasn't going to bless everything I touched just because I was a Christian and worked hard and smart.

Instead of blessing our farm experience, God actually used it to strip me. Maybe that's happened to you too. Maybe you took a job thinking you were going to do what your predecessors couldn't do. They didn't have the skills, faith, education, or "moxy" that you did. It would be different for you. You would have your department flying high in no time. But, to your surprise, you failed like the others, and you were back looking for a job.

Or maybe you invested in a relationship that people warned you about. You were convinced that you saw the good the others didn't see. Your love for them would work the magic that would transform them and produce a match made in heaven. But when that didn't happen you questioned God. Why didn't God come through for you? You had the best intentions.

I can relate.

Return from Exile

I was miserable during my time in exile, but in retrospect, I think God was saying,

> *I'm going to use you Remy, but when I use you I want you to know that it has nothing to do with YOU. It has everything to do with ME.*

Jeremiah's lament wasn't a total downer. Let's keep reading:

> But the Lord will not reject his people forever. Although he brings sorrow, he also has mercy and great love. He does not like to punish people or make them sad. Lamentations 3:31-33, NCV.

I've gone into exile and returned. Now I can say, with Jeremiah, *God doesn't reject his people forever. Although he brings sorrow, he also has mercy and great love.* I hope you can believe that and find comfort in your exile. One day you will also return.

What about you?

- *Do Jeremiah's words speak to you? If so, how?*

- *How has your exile experience stripped you?*

- *What are some bad attitudes that God has revealed to you in exile that need to go?*

Day Twenty

Comfort in Exile

*The LORD will surely comfort Zion and will look with compassion on all her ruins...*Isaiah 51:3

Once you see how many exile stories are in the Bible, the Bible becomes even more relevant. Many books in the Bible are written directly to exiles: to correct or comfort them.

The book of Isaiah is a good example of comfort spoken to exiles. God used Isaiah to tell his people that their time in exile was about over. God would soon show up to reveal his glory to people that had only known trouble:

>Comfort, comfort my people, says your God.
>Speak tenderly to Jerusalem, and proclaim to her

Return from Exile

that her hard service has been completed, that her sin has been paid for, that she has received from the LORD's hand double for all her sins.

A voice of one calling: "In the desert prepare the way for the LORD; make straight in the wilderness a highway for our God. Every valley shall be raised up, every mountain and hill made low; the rough ground shall become level, the rugged places a plain. And the glory of the LORD will be revealed, and all mankind together will see it. For the mouth of the LORD has spoken."
Isaiah 40:1-5

In other words, take courage people; your days of exile have an expiration date. They aren't meant to last forever. It's time to start looking for God to show up and bring you "home." This is good to know because exile makes you feel like a washout for God. All you can see is *your* failure, or what or whom has failed *you*.

Isaiah speaks to this hopelessness by communicating the restoration that God has for them:
> The LORD will surely comfort Zion and will look with compassion on all her ruins; he will make her deserts like Eden, her wastelands like the garden of the LORD. Joy and gladness will be found in her, thanksgiving and the sound of singing.

> "Listen to me, my people; hear me, my nation: The law will go out from me; my justice will become a light to the nations. My righteousness draws near speedily, my salvation is on the way, and my arm will bring justice to the nations.

The islands will look to me and wait in hope for my arm. Isaiah 51:3-5

If you are in the midst of exile, God's salvation might seem hard to believe. Maybe you looked for it for so long that you gave up. You conditioned yourself to no longer look for God. You've accepted "exile" as your lot in life. But don't be too quick to accept that role. Salvation might be closer than you think.

What about you?
- *Have you given up on God? Did your exile cause you to walk away, assuming God walked away first? Or do you still have hope of his return to rescue you? Why is that?*

- Read through the words of Isaiah 51 again. *What are the words he uses to describe exile? What are the words he uses to describe the restoration of God? Do any of these words feel like God might be speaking them to you?*

DAY TWENTY-ONE

Scattered Shame

Exile is a time of stripping, but when the stripping is done, restoration follows.

One of my favorite exile stories is hidden deep in the books of 2 Samuel and 1 Chronicles. The story is about King Saul's grandson, which is Jonathan's son. He's given two names. In 2 Samuel he's called, *Mephibosheth*, meaning: *he who scatters my shame.* In 1 Chronicles he's called, *Meribaal,* meaning: *the Lord is against me.* Two very contradictory names!

You have to piece together a few scriptures to make sense of the story. Here's the thumbnail storyline: Jonathan was the son of King Saul. David was next in line to become king. God chose David over the traditional choice of Jonathan, the king's son. In spite of this, Jonathan and David were friends, but Saul hated David. David and Jonathan made a covenant with each other. Jonathan promised to support David and protect him from Saul. David, in turn, promised to care for any of Jonathan's offspring should Jonathan be killed in battle.

Jonathan did soon die, along with his father, Saul. When that happened, Saul's entire family fled Jerusalem, convinced David would kill all of Saul's descendants (as was the custom of new kings). In the rush, Jonathan's five-year-old son was trampled and lost the use of his legs. He then lived for 20 years in the desert until David, now king, remembered his promise to Jonathan and invited his son to return.

My guess is that Jonathan's son went by the name "Meribaal" during the desert/exile season of his life. I'm sure it felt like *God was against him*. He went from being the grandson of the king, with all the preferential treatment that you'd expect, to an exile in the desert with no legs.

But his fortune turned when David sent for him. David spoke five blessings to Meribaal, which was most likely the cause for his name change to Mephibosheth (he who scatters my shame). As you listen to these words, consider how they might be words of blessing that God offers you as well (see 2 Samuel 9:6-13):

"Do not fear"
David didn't want Mephibosheth to fear retribution against his family. He wanted him to relax. In the same way, God wants to comfort you. He's not against you. He wants you to know that it doesn't matter what is in your

past. He accepts you unconditionally. It's easy to believe that life in exile will go from bad to worse. But God wants you to know that he has you in the palm of his hand.

"I will surely show you kindness."
It's one thing to not fear: to believe that bad things won't happen. But here, David assured Mephibosheth that good things *would* happen, even though the last twenty years hadn't been that way.

After you've been in exile a while, it's hard to believe that kindness is possible. You give up on having good days and start being grateful for the days that are *less* bad. But kindness is a core part of God's identity. You can expect to see that in various ways.

"I will restore all the land that belonged to your grandfather, Saul."
Here David reveals a specific kindness, the first of three. Imagine the wealth of King Saul. Imagine how much land he once owned. David gave all that land to Mephibosheth, an inheritance that he thought was lost forever.

Exile is a time of stripping, but when the stripping is done, restoration follows. That's something to look forward to. I can't promise that God will give you back exactly what you lost (a job, a marriage, finances, health, etc.) but he can restore good things to your life. Life *can* be good again.

"You will always eat at my table."
This is the second kindness David offered. To eat at the king's table was a great honor. Only family and

dignitaries were allowed that privilege. But that was offered to Mephibosheth, a former "enemy of the state," at least he assumed he was David's enemy.

In the same way, God honors us by offering us intimacy with him. We are now "friends of God" in spite of our past failure. God welcomes us into his presence and invites our prayers.

"I grant you all of Saul's servants."
David offered Mephibosheth one more kindness. Not only was Mephibosheth given Saul's land, but the servants to work the land. Although he still had no use of his legs, he was given the ability to overcome his setback.

In the same way, God wants to give you whatever you need to make a successful comeback. Exile is for a season. Don't let it become the norm.

Not long after Mephibosheth was welcomed into David's household, he married and experienced yet another kindness: a son named Micah, meaning: Who is like God? I'm sure that was the question Mephibosheth kept asking himself: *Who is like God? Who but God could bring me back from exile and restore me in such a dramatic way?* I bet he never dreamed that someone would marry him in his condition. But the grace of God allowed the impossible to happen...*above and beyond all he could ever hope or ask for.*

I hope this story brings some encouragement to you as you imagine how God might also scatter your shame and restore you to a new life, out of exile.

What about you?
- Review the five blessings mentioned. *Do any resonate with you? Could God be speaking these into your life?*

- *Is there anything blocking these blessings from your life?*

- Sometimes shame causes us to sabotage our restoration. *Is there anything you do, or attitude you hold, that might be blocking your restoration?*

- *What kindnesses has God shown you?*

DAY TWENTY-TWO

Exile Wisdom

...the beauty of having gone through an exile is when, after the stripping is over, you can truthfully say...I'm okay. I'm naked, but I'm okay.

I mentioned on Day Eighteen that God gives us companions in exile. God speaks to us words of comfort through people, certain Bible passages, and authors.[4] Today, I want to begin sharing a few readings from one of my exile "friends," Richard Rohr.

I had never heard of Rohr until a friend of mine recommended his book: *Falling Upward*. Since then I've been getting daily emails with excerpts from his many writings. I wish I would have known about Rohr earlier. His words cut to the essence of life and walking with God. Here is a reprint of a recent post from his blog:

Return from Exile

You Can't Make Love All Dressed Up
> We fear nothingness. That's why we fear death, of course, which feels like nothingness...The nothingness we fear so much is, in fact, the treasure and freedom that we long for, which is revealed in the joy and glory of the Risen Christ. We long for the space where there is nothing to prove and nothing to protect; where I am who I am, in the mind and heart of God, and that is more than enough... Spirituality teaches us to get naked ahead of time, so God can make love to us as we really are. Adapted from *Radical Grace: Daily Meditations*, p. 333[5]

"Getting naked" might be an odd way to put it, but isn't that what stripping is all about: getting naked? The pain of exile comes from the stripping that takes place. Not only does the stripping hurt; the fear of being naked and having nothing can be suffocating. But the beauty of having gone through an exile is when, after the stripping is over, you can truthfully say...*I'm okay. I'm naked, but I'm okay.*

What we feared isn't nearly the monster we thought it would be. Rohr says it's actually the treasure and freedom we long for, but have no idea how to attain it.

When I was a kid my parents fought about the lyrics to a song. It was called, "Is that all there is?" by Peggy Lee. The song listed a number of traumatic events, like your house burning down. The refrain was:
> *Is that all there is?*
> *If that's all there is my friends,*
>   *then let's keep dancing.*
> *Let's break out the booze and have a ball,*

F. Remy Diederich

if that's all there is.

My dad thought it was a stupid song because, of course, everyone would hate their house burning down. My mom saw the freedom of not being impacted by the tragedy. That's what we are talking about here.

Rohr says nakedness is that place where you have nothing to prove or protect. Once you've been exposed in your nakedness, that is, lost it all in exile and survived, you can stop playing that game. This is where you can "break out the booze and have a ball," so to speak.

I don't think we realize how much energy we put into acquiring status, protecting it, and pretending not to lose it. We want so much to be validated: to be told that we are doing a good job and that we matter. Wouldn't it be nice to let that all go?

I can't say that I've arrived at this place Rohr calls "nakedness," but I've had fleeting brushes with it. I know what's it's like to have nothing. There was a time when I was convinced that I would spend the rest of my life in poverty and out of ministry. But God met me in my weakness. I had nothing to offer him, yet he restored me and used me beyond what I ever imagined was possible.

So now, instead of working to "prove or protect," I'm just extremely grateful. If I lost it all tomorrow, I can't be sure, but I think I could "just keep dancing." At least I hope I would.

What about you?

- *Have you come to the freedom of "nakedness," or are you still in process?*

- *Does this idea of nakedness scare you, and if so, why?*

- *What is it about your exile that makes you feel "naked?"*

- *How have you resisted God's attempts to "strip" you?*

- *What needs to happen for you to let go of the fear of being "naked?"*

DAY TWENTY-THREE

The Two Halves of Life

One of the best-kept secrets, and yet one hidden in plain sight, is that the way up is the way down. - Richard Rohr

Richard Rohr often speaks of the "two halves of life." The first half is spent creating a box: rules to live by, unchangeable truths to help you feel in control, and markers that show success. He says these are all a natural part of development, a phase we all go through: like training wheels on a bicycle.

But the second half of life is meant to let go of these constructs. By letting go of the box you are free to experience life in its fullness. You are no longer threatened by what's outside of the box. Your thinking becomes less black and white: less in or out (he calls this kind of polarizing: *dualism*). You are less inclined to put a value judgment on everything and choose to just experience life as it is.

But Rohr says that to transition to the second half of life requires an exile: a time of stripping. It often feels unsuccessful and contrary to everything you've worked so hard to achieve in the first half of life. Here is another post where he refers to the second half of life.

The Two Halves of Life
> The soul has many secrets. They are only revealed to those who want them, and are never completely forced upon us. One of the best-kept secrets, and yet one hidden in plain sight, is that the way up is the way down. Or, if you prefer, the way down is the way up.
>
> In Scripture, we see that the wrestling and wounding of Jacob are necessary for Jacob to become Israel (Genesis 32:26-32), and the death and resurrection of Jesus are necessary to create Christianity. The loss and renewal pattern is so constant and ubiquitous that it should hardly be called a secret at all.
>
> Yet it is still a secret, probably because we do not want to see it. We do not want to embark on a further journey (the second half of life) if it feels like going down, especially after having put so much sound and fury into going up (the first half of life). This is surely the first and primary reason why many people never get to the fullness of their own lives. Adapted from *Falling Upward: A Spirituality for the Two Halves of Life.*

Exile can produce much fear. But the fear comes from feeling the loss of what you think life MUST BE. We are afraid we won't achieve our goals, and if we reach them, we fear losing what we've gained. We resist any downward movement, but if Rohr is right, down is the way up.

If you can see good, even in downward movement, then you've won! You have nothing to fear. Nothing can stop you. You are a winner either way! Suddenly, exile is viewed as an *opportunity* to a fuller life.

What about you?
- *What is the box from the first half of your life that has kept you contained?*

- *What are some good things about the box? What are some bad things about it?*

Return from Exile

- *What do you fear losing in life?*

- *How could (or has) exile enable/d you to experience life more fully?*

DAY TWENTY-FOUR

The Enemy of the Good

We grow spiritually much more by doing it wrong than by doing it right. – Richard Rohr

The value of exile isn't readily understandable. It takes time to sink in. But once it sinks in, everything starts to make sense...at least from a faith perspective. I hope that after twenty-three days you are gaining some understanding in this experience called "exile."

The problem many Christians have with exile is they try to understand it through a secular grid of success. It doesn't work. We should have caught on to that when Jesus said, "The last will be first and the first will be last." But no one wants to believe that. We want to think Jesus was being clever. No, he was speaking Truth; we are just too blind to see it.

Return from Exile

Exile will always be offensive until we understand life from God's perspective. Here is yet another post taken from Richard Rohr's book, *Falling Upward:*

The Demand for the Perfect is the Enemy of the Good
We grow spiritually much more by doing it wrong than by doing it right. That might just be the central message of how spiritual growth happens, yet nothing in us wants to believe it.

If there is such a thing as human perfection, it seems to emerge precisely from how we handle the imperfection that is everywhere, especially our own. What a clever place for God to hide holiness, so that only the humble and earnest will find it! A "perfect" person ends up being one who can consciously forgive and include imperfection rather than one who thinks he or she is totally above and beyond imperfection.

It becomes sort of obvious once you say it out loud. In fact, I would say that *the demand for the perfect is the greatest enemy of the good.* Perfection is a mathematical or divine concept; goodness is a beautiful human concept that includes us all. People whom we call "good people" are always people who have learned how to include contradictions and others, even at risk to their own proper self-image or their social standing. This is quite obvious in Jesus.
Adapted from *Falling Upward: A Spirituality for the Two Halves of Life*, p. xxii-xxiii

Rohr is on to something here. Let me try to unpack it. Exile feels so bad because we insist on life being perfect.

We expect things to go "well." We all expect to execute "Plan A," which typically includes graduating from high school and college, getting a good job, getting married, raising a family, and finding financial independence before dying in our sleep at 95. If Plan A doesn't happen, something must be wrong. Fix it! We feel defeated if we fall short of our goals, or what we might call, "perfection." Then we are hard on ourselves as well as others whom we perceive as failures.

But in this kind of success matrix, what do we do with failure? Where does it fit? Or do we just do all we can to avoid it, or deny it should it happen? If we can't deny it, then must we judge it harshly and promise that it will never happen again?

Sometimes the only way to break free from this "success" mentality is to experience "failure." It can actually be a gift to "fail" so that you wake up the next day and see that the world didn't end. Life goes on. God is still God. The forecasts were wrong: there is life after failure, unless you insist on living in regret.

Rohr gives a twist to the idea of perfection saying: *A "perfect" person ends up being one who can consciously forgive and include imperfection rather than one who thinks he or she is totally above and beyond imperfection.* Did you catch that? The perfect person is able to include imperfection in their world. Can you do that, or does everything and everyone in your world need to hit the mark?

How do you come to this place of "perfection?" Through failure. Until you fail you live under the delusion that you've "got it" and others should too. Until you fail you talk about grace but don't live it, or offer it to others. It's only a theory. It's your theology, not your practice. But exile strips you of this delusion and grants you the ability to receive grace so you can, in turn, offer it to other failures.

What about you?
- *How have you grown spiritually by doing it wrong? How so?*

- *How has the perfect been the enemy of the good for you?*

- *What is it about failure that enables you to offer grace to others?*

DAY TWENTY-FIVE

The Discipline of Darkness

When you are in the dark, listen, and God will give you a very precious message for someone else when you get into the light. - Oswald Chambers

I've mentioned how Richard Rohr has been a traveling companion for me. Another companion has been Oswald Chambers from his devotional, *My Utmost for His Highest.* In it he talks about exile as a discipline of darkness:

> At times God puts us through the discipline of darkness to teach us to heed Him. Song birds are taught to sing in the dark, and we are put into the shadow of God's hand until we learn to hear Him...

Have you seen your exile as that...*a discipline*...a time of intense teaching or training? Or has it just been a time of disappointment?

When you are in the dark, the darkness shrouds what once held your attention. When a small candle is lit in darkness, the candle becomes the focus while everything else fades to black. That's exactly what God wants to accomplish in exile. He wants his light to become your focal point while everything else in your life is diminished.

Exile is meant to help you *detach* from everything that is unnecessary in your life so you will *attach* yourself fully to God. As you attach yourself to God you can let go of the things you felt were so important to your survival.

It's one thing to talk about God and faith. It's another thing to live it. Exile helps you live out what you've been talking about for years. If there was a better way to effect this change, God would use it. But there's not.

In the book of Hebrews, the writer refers to the priest in Genesis that met Abraham (Melchizedek). He had his own special "discipline of darkness."

> Without father or mother, without genealogy, without beginning of days or end of life, resembling the Son of God, he remains a priest forever. Just think how great he was: Even the patriarch Abraham gave him a tenth of the plunder! Hebrews 7:3,4

What made this priest like Jesus? It's not in what he had but in what he lacked. Read these verses again and notice all the negatives: without, without, without.. Melchizedek was without everything that typically gives one their identity: mother, father, and genealogy. His only identity was as a priest of God. Because of it, he was called "great," and Abraham felt compelled to bless him with a tenth of his best possessions. Are you willing to undergo that kind of a stripping to obtain that same identity with God?

The apostle Paul was. He said he lost everything when he followed Jesus but he gained an intimate knowledge of him. He talks here about what he gained from his suffering:
> But whatever were gains to me I now consider loss for the sake of Christ. What is more, I consider everything a loss because of the surpassing worth of knowing Christ Jesus my Lord, for whose sake I have lost all things. I consider them garbage, that I may gain Christ. Philippians 3:7,8

The purpose of exile is to help us gain this kind of single mindedness.

Oswald Chambers offers this final insight:
> Are you in the dark just now in your circumstances, or in your life with God? When you are in the dark, listen, and God will give you a very precious message for someone else when you get into the light. Oswald Chambers, April 21, *My Utmost For His Highest*

What about you?
- *How does this land on you? Are Chamber's words hopeful or does it just make you shake your head and say, "Right now I'm not concerned about having a precious message for someone else. I'd*

just like to make it through one day happy?" Be honest.

- *What is it that God might be teaching you in the darkness that you could share one day in the light?*

- *Are you willing to be like Jesus in what you lack?* Paul lost everything and counted it a privilege so that he might know Christ. *What have you lost and would you say that your losses have helped you to know Christ?*

DAY TWENTY-SIX

Facing Your Nakedness

Exile forces the question: do you need anything more than God to be fulfilled and happy?

Exile exposes you at the core of your being. As I've already said, it strips you, leaving you naked. Exile forces you to confront who you really are, warts and all. Let's explore this a little more.

Nakedness is not a very attractive condition for most of us. Clothes are good for many reasons! They hide what we lack and project a positive image regardless of what is underneath. When the clothes come off and you face your nakedness, (without the trophies, achievements, resumes, or accolades from those you respect) can you live with the person you see? Can you feel as good about *that* person as you can when all your clothes are on and

Return from Exile

you are *lookin' good?*

To be stripped of our "clothes" can be devastating because so much of our identity is tied up in them. We *need* them to survive...at least that is what we often think. But exile forces the question: do you need anything more than God to be fulfilled and happy? Is all your talk about God being your "everything" genuine, or is it just one more article of clothing that you put on to make you feel valuable and acceptable to others?

When we face our physical nakedness in the mirror, we typically note how we have too much of this and not enough of that. We are desperate to modify our body in order to be found acceptable by others. It's the same way emotionally. Without the "clothing" of performance there is so much self-blame and regret. Just listen to the accusations of your inner voice: *How could you let this happen? You are such a fool. This is what dad warned you about. This will never change. It's only going to get worse and you can't fix it. You had your chance. God is finished with you now...*and on and on it goes. Most of us find coping mechanisms to cover up these voices.

As hard as it is to "get naked," we won't ever know our true worth until everything is removed. It's only in the depths of our failure that God can prove his unconditional love for us. Sadly, too few of us are willing to make ourselves that vulnerable and so we are never sure of our acceptance with God (or people, for that matter).

But Paul made himself that vulnerable. He said that everything apart from Jesus died to him:
> I have been crucified with Christ and I no longer

live, but Christ lives in me. Galatians 2:20

Jesus made up for everything that he lost. Jesus clothed him in a way that his performance never could.

What about you?
- *How does it feel to think of your weaknesses being fully exposed in front of people you respect? God?*

- *What do you imagine people saying to you about your weaknesses? What would God say?*

- *Can you identify with Paul's words about being crucified with Christ? If so, how?*

Day Twenty-Seven

Return from Exile

*Naming your loss "exile" gives you permission
to look at loss with fresh eyes.*

We have spent twenty-six days "in exile," at least, talking about it. It's time to head home. In the remaining days I want to give you some practical ideas on how to find your way out of exile. The first step out of exile is to simply name it.

Throughout this book I've referred to the experience of loss as: *exile*. That's probably a new term to you, at least used in a new way. Last year I spoke about exile at my home church. Someone stopped me and said, "Thank you for this series," assuming I knew what she meant. I asked why she liked it and she said, "I guess it just helps to have a name for what I've been going through."

That's true, isn't it? It's like going to the doctor when you are sick and they tell you you've got the latest Asian flu. There's nothing you can do about it, but somehow it helps to give it a name. It helps to know that you aren't abnormal or imagining things. What you've got is common to all people and you'll eventually get over it. This is called "normalizing." You thought your experience was unique until you realize it is what most people experience. It's normal.

For example, last spring I suddenly lost my energy. I didn't know what was wrong. There were a few Sunday's that I couldn't stand to speak at church so I sat through my sermons. Before I spoke I felt so depleted I just wanted to cry. I had all the blood tests done but nothing was found.

In Wisconsin, when you can't find a diagnosis, people assume it must be Lyme's disease...a disease brought on by being bitten by deer ticks. So I started researching Lyme's, anxiously to find a solution. It really bothered me to not KNOW what was wrong. I remember thinking; *I don't care what I have. I just want to know what it is so I can deal with it.*[6]

That's how we feel emotionally too. We want to know what's wrong, so it helps to have a name for what we experience. Technically, what I've been referring to as "exile" is what most people would call "grief and loss." But most people think that someone has to die to grieve so they never think to apply grief remedies to their loss. Naming your loss "exile" gives you permission to look at loss with fresh eyes. Plus, there are many biblical examples of exile to reflect on to gain insight.

Return from Exile

Now that you have a name for your loss, you can do something about it. You can find a map that will help you to return from exile. We'll talk about that in coming days.

What about you?
- *Have you ever been concerned about physical symptoms that didn't have a diagnosis?*

- *Describe the helplessness of not knowing what's wrong.*

- *Does it help you to have a name for the loss you've experienced? How so?*

- *Are you hopeful that you will find your way out of exile?*

Day Twenty-Eight

Grieve Your Loss

Depression happens when you believe the lie:
Life will never be good again.

Once you name your loss, the next thing to do is grieve it. As straightforward as this may seem, we rarely grieve our losses. We get too caught up in other aspects of our loss. We might spend time blaming others, regretting mistakes, fixing problems, or wandering around disillusioned. We overlook the obvious: we had expectations for life that weren't met. That's a loss. Losses hurt. If we want to resolve the hurt we need to give ourselves permission to feel the pain of the loss and grieve it.

Let me walk you through what grieving your loss means. The grief cycle was first created to describe what happens when you lose someone to death.[7] But these stages are true for any loss:

Stage One: Denial
Your first reaction to loss is to minimize or ignore the loss so you don't feel the full pain of it. You hope you'll wake up some day and find it didn't happen or what happened doesn't affect you. If you are unable to ignore the loss on your own, you might look for help by immersing yourself in things like: travel, a relationship, a hobby, exercise, drugs and alcohol, religion, blaming others, escaping responsibility, etc.

Stage Two: Anger
When you come out of denial, you realize the loss still exists. It hasn't gone anywhere and that leads to anger. You thought you could out-fox the loss with denial. But it waited for you. It's right there, staring you in the face. If you've never dealt with the loss, anger is the natural response. The tricky thing here is that we don't always connect our anger to the true loss. We might focus on a current problem, thinking that's why we are angry, when, in reality, it's a distant un-grieved loss.

Stage Three: Bargaining
Bargaining is when you try to take the short-cut to overcome your loss. You might plead with God to let someone live by saying you'll be more spiritual. You might promise your spouse you'll do better if he or she won't divorce you. You might try a network-marketing scheme or a lottery ticket to get out of a financial jam. Bargaining is an act of desperation to keep you from experiencing the full effect of your loss.

Stage Four: Depression
When bargaining fails, depression sets in. Depression happens when you believe the lie: *Life will never be good again*. The power of this lie is that it's close to the truth. It makes sense. If you lost something significant to your joy, then how can life ever be good again? The truth is...life may never be the *same*...but life can be good again, *just different*. It's a faith issue because it requires believing God can do this in your life; that God is good and wants to bring fullness back to your life. If you can't believe in God or his goodness, it's easy to slip into terminal despair.

Stage Five: Acceptance
Here you fully accept the new you and believe that God is with you and for you. You believe that life *can* be good again. You are not the same person you were before the loss. The old you died in exile and a new you has been resurrected to live a new life. But even though you are not the same, you are no less of a person. You are just different. *Life* is different.

Many people refuse to come to this place. They fight it. They dig in their heels. They don't want to be different. They just want their old life back. They think denial, anger, and bargaining will help so they stay stuck in the past. But these tactics won't help. Accepting the new you is the only way to bring true peace back to your life.

Grieving your loss is a process. It takes time. There is no quick fix. Let grief do its work in you.

What about you?
- *Where are you at in the grief cycle?*

Return from Exile

- *Where have you gotten stuck? Why is that?*

- *Do you believe that life will ever be good again? Why or why not?*

- *What will it take to get you unstuck?*

- *What is it about the "new you" that scares you?*

- *What makes you hopeful?*

Day Twenty-Nine

Listen

To be told to "be quiet and listen" is almost offensive to people who expect a solution to every problem.

I live about a mile from a freeway. I don't think much about it. I rarely hear the cars. But some days in the summer, if I sit outside, I'm quiet, and think about it, there it is. I hear it. It's the constant hum of the freeway.

I hear a lot of things in my backyard when I'm quiet. For example: if I focus on birdcalls, I hear all kinds of birds I didn't even know were out there. That's what happens when you stop to listen: you hear things you don't normally hear.

If you want to return from exile, learn to be quiet and listen. That's hard to do because there is so much

Return from Exile

"chatter" going on in the mind. There are so many things to think about regarding your situation. You think about all of the:
- embarrassing mistakes you made causing you to end up in exile.
- people who did you wrong and the ways you hope they get paid back.
- worst case scenarios and how life will never be good again.
- the gossip being spread about your situation.
- questions you have about why God didn't rescue you from your problems.
- comeback plans that never worked out.
- schemes to get your life back on track.

With all of that going on in your mind, it's hard to be quiet. Sometimes we call our obsessive thinking "prayer" because we direct a lot of our thinking at God. I'm not so sure it's prayer if it's just you venting without giving God equal time to speak back.

If you want to return from exile it's important to learn the discipline of silence. Turn off your obsessive thoughts. Stop judging yourself and others. Stop planning and scheming. Stop regretting. Just shut it all down and create space in your mind for new thoughts.

Researchers say that 90% of our thoughts every day are the same as the day before.[8] We just keep rehashing them. We need to cease thinking to create space for new thoughts: *better thoughts.*

Richard Rohr talks about silence as a form of prayer:
> Prayer is largely just being silent: holding the tension instead of even talking it through,

offering the moment instead of fixing it by words and ideas, loving reality as it is instead of understanding it fully. Prayer is commonly a willingness to say "I don't know." We must not push the river, we must just trust that we are already in the river, and God is the certain flow and current. *The Freedom of Not Knowing.*[9]

Sometimes we try too hard to fix our situation. We are desperate to gain back control. But maybe that's one of the big reasons we end up in exile: God wants to show us that we are not in control. He is. Rohr continues to explain...

...the way of faith is not the way of efficiency. So much of life is just a matter of listening and waiting ...It is like carrying and growing a baby: women wait and trust and hopefully eat good food, and the baby is born.

To be told to "be quiet and listen" is almost offensive to people who expect a solution to every problem. But God has some things to share that he can only share with you in silence. You don't want to miss out.

What about you?
- *How good are you at silence and listening? What thoughts keep you from it?*

- *What can you do to create that kind of space in your life?*

Day Thirty

Admit

Why is it so hard to admit what is so plain to others?

If you are quiet and listen to God, you will most likely hear from him. Really. But you might not like what you hear. God has a way of shedding light on areas of your life that you thought were well-hidden or even non-existent. The best thing you can do is agree with him. Admit your faults. It stings at first, but it's the fast track out of exile.

Instead of admitting, some people choose to ignore what is plain to everyone else. Isn't that true? You meet someone and, in just a matter of minutes, discern a character defect. Their flaws are no secret to anyone but them. Surprisingly, what you saw in minutes, they have defended, excused, or ignored for decades. Why is it so hard to admit what is so plain to others?

A few months back I was preparing my Sunday message. I wrote in the text: "I'm a bit of a workaholic." I was going to laugh when I said it, a little chuckle to show my guilty pleasure of nursing a habit I know is wrong, yet prized in our culture.

But God convicted me that I was making light of a problem I have always had. I'm not a "bit" of a workaholic. I AM a workaholic, in recovery just like any addict. Either it's wrong or it's not. I can't cover it with a knowing laugh and hope people look the other way. But that's what we do isn't it? Rather than change, we put all kinds of defense mechanisms in place thinking that we've got people fooled. They are not.

When God apprehended the apostle Paul, striking him with blindness, his quick response was: "What would you have me to do?"[10] He immediately recognized that his blindness was an exile given by God to reveal to him what he was unwilling to see on his own.

In the same way, the story of Samson tells how he lived his whole life blind to his selfishness and greed until the Philistines burned his eyes out of his sockets. Ironically, only after losing his eyes did he see what had been wrong with him his entire life.[11]

My guess is you actually know what is wrong in your life. You just haven't been willing to admit it. If you truly can't see, then David's prayer might help you:
> Search me, God, and know my heart; test me and know my anxious thoughts. See if there is any offensive way in me, and lead me in the way

Return from Exile

everlasting. Psalm 139:23,24

God knows you inside and out. He knows what needs addressing in your life and is happy to show you if you are willing to admit to what he shows you.

You might also want to invite trusted people to give you feedback to help you discover your blind spots. However it happens, you need to own up to whatever is wrong inside of you.

What about you?
- *What keeps you from admitting your character defects?*

- *What can you do to find the courage to fully admit them and begin the healing process?*

- *What do you think God is after that you have refused to admit?* Write it down. Now tell someone.

Day Thirty-One

Face Your Shame

Shame is a deep sense of worthlessness and inadequacy that feels irresolvable. It is one of the reasons people never return from exile.

Once you've admitted your issues, it's tempting to return to denial. This happens because admitting your flaws often leads to a sense of hopelessness: you become overwhelmed at the size of the problem and convinced that there is no solution.

In my book, *Healing the Hurts of Your Past*, I call this hopelessness: shame. Shame is a deep sense of worthlessness and inadequacy that feels irresolvable. It is one of the reasons people never return from exile.

Shame is rooted in the lies we believe, lies like:

Return from Exile

I don't deserve to return from exile,
I deserve to be punished.
I don't measure up. My family, my company,
my church are all better off without me.
I don't have what it takes to succeed at work,
in ministry, as a parent, or in marriage.
I don't have what it takes to recover
from the trauma of losing a loved one.
My cancer, divorce, firing, bankruptcy, etc.
are more than I can overcome.
Failure is my true self. I have no hope of change.

Shame feeds off these lies and creates new ones, trapping you in an ever-increasing web of lies. Once you believe them, they become your new reality. They define your existence, causing you to sabotage any success that God might bring your way.

If you want to get out of exile, you have to confront your lies. The biggest lie we are tempted to believe is that our value comes from what we do: our performance. As long as you believe that, you will remain in exile because you will never be good enough to return. You will never be the perfect wife, husband, parent, employee, friend, child, athlete, artist, or whatever the standard is that hangs over your head. If achieving perfection is the standard necessary to leave exile, you are stuck.

But the truth is: your value doesn't come from *what you do*. Your value comes from *whose you are*. You are God's child. This is your identity. Your value comes from what God thinks of you, not what you achieve in life. So here are six truths to help reshape your self-concept:

1. **God created you.** This fact alone gives you infinite worth. Your value comes from being created by a perfect God. Everything that comes from God is good. Genesis 1:27,31

2. **God loves you.** God loves what he creates. It's impossible for God to not love what he creates because everything he creates is an extension of himself and therefore has infinite worth. John 3:16

3. **God accepts you.** He welcomes you into his presence. He wants you in his presence so much that he sent Jesus to make it possible. John 15:15

4. **God forgives you.** God washes you of every sin you've ever committed, thought about committing, or might commit in coming days. He has removed any reason you think he might have for rejecting you. Psalm 103:12

5. **God approves you.** Since God forgives you, that means you are as perfect in his eyes as Jesus himself. You have a clean slate. There is no sin greater than God's forgiveness. You can't out sin God's forgiveness, so that means you stand before him fully approved. The Bible calls this being declared righteous. Romans 3:21,22

6. **God empowers you.** God not only put you in right standing with him, he gifts you with the presence of his Spirit to help you live a new life. Ephesians 1:13,14, Romans 8:9,10

Focusing your mind on these truths will help you to stand strong, whether you are in exile or not.

What about you?
- *What are the inadequacies that you are most conscious of having?*

- *Do you hate yourself for these inadequacies? If so, why?*

- *Could it be that you've been stuck in exile so long because you don't like yourself very much and you feel the need to punish yourself for it?* Think about that before you are quick to discount it.

- *How could embracing these six truths help you thrive in exile and return from it?*

Day Thirty-Two

Peace in the Pain

Peace doesn't come from ... having God fix what's broken.
Peace comes by being fixed on God.

Exile can be a raw existence where nothing is settled, and it *feels* like it never will be. Peace is a distant memory. But Jesus said he came to give us peace:

> Peace I leave with you; my peace I give you. I do not give to you as the world gives. Do not let your hearts be troubled and do not be afraid. John 14:27

Notice that the peace Jesus gives isn't the peace that we find in the world. Peace in the world is the moment when all is calm. No problems. No worries. No conflict. The peace that Jesus offers is a peace that comes *even in the midst of trouble.* It's the calm that exists in the eye of

a storm. God helps us better understand his peace when he said:
> If only you had paid attention to my commands, your peace would have been like a river, your well-being like the waves of the sea. Isaiah 48:18

What does a river have in common with waves of the sea? They both run on indefinitely. God is saying: if his people would have aligned themselves with Him their peace would be unending. They would have been able to rise above their problems.

Combining the thoughts of Jesus and Isaiah...the peace of the world is temporary and conditional. The peace of God is unconditional and, therefore, never stops. That means our peace doesn't have to depend on our circumstances. We can have peace of mind even when our world crumbles around us.

The average person loses peace when they experience one of three things: change, conflict, or disappointment. In other words, when they lose control. When a person loses control they usually work their way through these four plans:
- Plan A: they take back control by whatever means necessary.
- Plan B: if they can't take back control, they ask or pay someone else to do it for them.
- Plan C: if Plans A & B fail, they go into denial by ignoring, minimizing, or escaping their pain in some way.
- Plan D: if none of these work, they ask God to fix it.
- If all plans fail, they fall into despair.

Sound familiar? In one sense, there's nothing wrong with this process. It's natural. Sometimes we need our plans to fail to see God work. But it's important to realize that God doesn't always answer Plan D prayers (*Fix it! Get me out of this jam!*) because that's the peace of the world. He wants us to experience a peace that is better than that, a peace that transcends our circumstances.

Peace doesn't come by getting God to bring all your chaos under your control. Peace comes when you bring all of your chaos to God and place it under his control. In fact, Isaiah tells God:
> You will keep in perfect peace all who trust in you, whose thoughts are fixed on you! Isaiah 26:3, New Living Translation

Notice the source of peace. Peace doesn't come from taking control or having God fix what's broken. Peace comes by being *fixed on God.*

My point is that returning from exile should never be your goal so you can get your old life back, or "just be happy again." Exile *is your life* for a season. Your goal shouldn't be to escape it but embrace it. God wants to meet you in your exile and help you to experience peace and joy *there,* not hold your breath and run through this season hoping to exhale on the other side. Clamoring for premature peace will only abort the process that God brought you into exile to experience.

You see, how you handle loss is at the heart of what it means to be spiritual. Most people fail this test miserably. They live their life resenting their loss and trying to deny it. But Jesus came into the world to do

Return from Exile

more than die for our sins. He came into the world to show us how to overcome loss and suffering. He showed us how to embrace our loss (the cross) and overcome it (the resurrection). When you finally see this and the light bulb goes off in your brain, you are ready to return from exile.

No matter what you might be suffering today, God has a peace to "guard your heart and mind" (as Paul promised the Philippian church – 4:7). If you can experience the peace of God in exile, you can experience it anywhere.

What about you?
- *What is your process to take back control in your life?*

- *Can you relate Plans A,B,C and D that I laid out above? How so?*

- *Have you been asking God to bring control to your life rather than bringing your life under his control? What can you do to turn that around?*

Day Thirty-Three

Be the Hero

Healthy stories challenge us to be active characters, not passive victims or observers. - John Trent

When you are stuck in exile there comes a time to "be the hero" of your story. A negative way to say this: *stop playing the victim.*

It doesn't take any courage to be angry about your situation. It doesn't take any skill to complain, gossip, cast blame, or feel sorry for yourself. Anyone can do that. But is that the story you want your life to tell?

Would you watch a movie for two hours about a person who suffered an injustice, then complained about it, and felt sorry for himself the rest of the movie? Of course not! What makes a good story is when someone faces loss or injustice with wisdom, courage, and grace to *overcome* it. We call these people heroes. So why not be the hero of your own story?

Being the hero requires a choice: a heroic choice. It means stepping up and saying, *I'm not going to let my past experiences control me anymore. I'm not going to let my present circumstances define me. I'm going to take responsibility for what's happened to me and move on with my life. This won't defeat me!*

Heroic choices free you from getting stuck in exile and open your life up to new possibilities. They make your story compelling. Engaging. I like what John Trent says about the power good choices have on your life:

> Healthy stories challenge us to be active characters, not passive victims or observers. Both the present and the future are determined by choices, and choice is the essence of character. If we see ourselves as active characters in our own stories, we can exercise our human freedom to choose a present and future for ourselves and for those we love that give life meaning. *Choosing to Live the Blessing.*

Trent makes the case that we should be proactive in choosing our future and not let our future simply happen to us. He builds on this idea of choice when he says:

> We can curse the past like victims of circumstance, or we can bless it like victors over our circumstances. It's up to us. It's our choice. In some of the strongest and most compelling stories, the main character makes life-and-death choices. These choices give the story energy.

They make the plot intriguing. They also change the character.

The character who doesn't make choices is weak and passive. So if we want our lives to tell strong and compelling stories in which the characters grow into people of blessing, then we – the characters – have to make choices. Choices that are sometimes difficult. Choices that are sometimes painful. Choices that are sometimes critical, where something important is at stake.

If you think of the movies that touch you, they most often reach a moment of decision for the protagonist. In the beginning of the story she struggles with a problem, but there is a "make or break" moment. Against all odds she decides to take a risk and do the right thing.

The risk adds tension to the story because it adds a level of doubt. *Can she do it? Will she regret her choice?* In the end her choice pays off. You breathe a sigh of relief. Her choice enables her to overcome her struggle and become the hero. That's a story you are willing to pay money to see.

Think of your life as a story half written. Half the book is full. You can't do anything about those early chapters. But the rest of your book has all blank pages. *You determine how your story will end. What will you write?*

Remember, the most compelling stories are turn-around stories…stories where a person was down for the count and made a comeback…even in the eleventh hour. So never give up on your story. Ask God to help you write a compelling comeback story.

What about you?
- *How have you allowed your past experiences and present circumstances to control your story?*

- *What people have you allowed to control your story?*

- *Are you currently making choices that will tell a good story?*

- *What are some choices you can make this week that will make you the hero of your story?*

- *Do you believe that you can make a comeback from your exile? Why or why not?*

- *How does God play into your comeback story?*

Day Thirty-Four

Reframing the Loss

Reframing enables you to be thankful for thankless situations.

In the book, *Change or Die*, Alan Deutchman says there are three factors that contribute to change: relationships, retraining, and reframing. Change requires the right person coaching you (relationship), the right information (retraining), and to see your problem from a fresh perspective (reframing).

All three of these components are also important if you want to return from exile. Most people think that just getting good information will help (retraining). We buy self-help books for this reason. Some people realize the importance of that catalytic counselor, friend, or pastor who made the difference in their change (relationship).

But what we often lack is the right perspective (reframing). The information and relationships don't help if you don't have the right perspective to actively reinforce the needed change.

The term "reframing" comes from the idea that you can often change the meaning of a picture by adjusting the frame. Imagine a picture of people enjoying a beach, but there is a storm building in the distance. You can put the frame around the storm and call it a terrible day. Or you can put the frame around the beach scene and see the joy of it. It's all in the framing.

There is an example of the apostle Paul reframing his experience in a letter he wrote to the Corinthian church in Greece. The church was encountering great persecution for its faith. Paul too had suffered greatly. He relates to them his perspective on his personal "exile:"

> God...comforts us in all our troubles, so that we can comfort those in any trouble with the comfort we ourselves have received from God...In our hearts we felt the sentence of death. But this happened that we might not rely on ourselves but on God, who raises the dead. See 2 Corinthians 1:3-10

Paul reframed his suffering as an *opportunity* to learn how to be comforted by God so he might pour out the same comfort to others that suffer. He refused to play the victim, complain, or feel sorry for himself. He trusted there was a greater good that God had for him, even if he couldn't see it.

Did you notice what he added about the "God who

raises the dead?" That's key to his reframing. Every person in exile needs to believe that God is a god of resurrection. That means you believe God can do anything at any moment to turn around your life.

Reframing enables you to be thankful for seemingly thankless situations. I just finished watching a documentary on Steve Jobs. The narrator mentioned how Jobs softened as he aged. When asked why that was, Jobs said: *Failure.* His failures made him a better person, and for that he was thankful. I'm sure he didn't see failure as a blessing when it first happened. That took reframing his experiences.

When TIME magazine remembered Nelson Mandela,[12] they quoted his response when asked what happened to him after 25 years in jail. He said, "*I matured.*" That was his chance to vent his hatred and resentment to the world for the injustice done to him. That was his chance to tell the world how his captors ruined his life, robbing him of his right to happiness. But like Jobs, Mandela was able to see the value in a time of exile by reframing his experience. He took control of his story and used the injustice to shape him into the leader his country desperately needed.

What about you?
- *How can you reframe the exile that you are in?*

- *What is it that God is working in you (or wants to) that you can start receiving and thanking him for today?*

Day Thirty-Five

Reframing Your Offender

People who refuse to forgive...think they have taken back control, but in reality their world has gotten smaller.

In addition to learning how to reframe your loss, it's also important to reframe anyone who has caused you to enter exile, that is, your offender.

Reframing your offender involves forgiveness. We often frame our offender as the winner in a conflict. We frame them as the one in control, while we are the one who is powerless: the loser. These pictures need to change.

When we've been offended, we mistakenly think anger and resentment toward our offender is a means to balance the power deficit. They hurt us so we hold them in contempt. We refuse to forgive them unless they fulfill our demands.

But instead of giving us control, our resentment gives our offender control over us. As long as we think they owe us, we are obligated to resent them. This only prolongs our time in exile. What we need is to be free from any anger or resentment toward our offender. We obtain this freedom by forgiving.

Forgiveness doesn't excuse the offense. It simply frees you from the need to provide payback of any kind. It enables you to close the book on the past chapters of your life and give your full attention to the present moment and the future. Isn't it bad enough that your offender stole from you? Do you really want to give them more space in your brain, even for a minute?

Miraslov Volf describes forgiveness as absorbing wrong. He says:
> Hanging on the cross, Jesus provided the ultimate example of his command to replace the principle of retaliation ("an eye for an eye and a tooth for a tooth") with the principle of nonresistance ("if anyone strikes you on the right cheek, turn the other also") (Matthew 5:38-42).
>
> By suffering violence as an innocent victim, he took upon himself the aggression of the persecutors. He broke the vicious cycle of violence by absorbing it, taking it upon himself. He refused to be sucked into the automatism of revenge... *Exclusion and Embrace*

Jesus broke the cycle of violence by absorbing wrong

like a dry sponge absorbs water. Like a running back absorbs the linebacker's hit, and continues on to score a touchdown, forgiveness absorbs injustice to overcome it. Absorbing the pain of injustice seems impossible, but it can be done with God's help.

People who refuse to forgive think in terms of scarcity. In their mind, they've lost something that can't be replaced. They are forever at a loss and their only play, in response to their loss, is to ward off future attacks with anger and various forms of payback. They want to protect what's left of them.

But with this response, they don't realize what they've done to themselves. They might think they have taken back control, but in reality their world has gotten smaller. They have sent themselves farther into exile, maybe to never return.

A faith-filled person doesn't think in terms of scarcity but rather abundance. They believe in a God who can fill up whatever was lost by any offense. He can even raise the dead. By reframing their offender, the faith-filled person absorbs the losses of life and is free to leave their exile.

Here is a shocking example of someone's ability to reframe their loss from a worst-case scenario. The following words were found on a wrapping paper in the Ravensbrück concentration camp:

> Lord, remember not only the men and women of good will, but also those of ill will. But do not remember all the suffering they have inflicted upon us. Remember rather the fruits we brought, thanks

to this suffering: our comradeship, our loyalty, our humility, the courage, the generosity, the greatness of heart that has grown out of this. And when they come to judgment, let all the fruits we have borne be their forgiveness. *Cries of the Heart*[13]

What about you?
- *Could unforgiveness be keeping you in exile? How might that be true?*

If forgiveness is an issue for you, there are many posts on my blog at readingremy.com addressing this. My book, STUCK...*how to overcome your anger and reclaim your life*, takes an in-depth look at forgiveness as well.

For another example of reframing, see the appendix: "The Gift of Cancer."

Day Thirty-Six

Reframing your Identity

*If you insist on clinging to old identities,
you will never be able to receive the new identity,
life, and experiences God has for you.*

What often keeps people stuck in exile is a loss of identity. The loss they experience in exile is so disillusioning they don't know who they are any more. Therefore, in addition to reframing your loss and your offender, it's also important to reframe your identity if you want to return from exile.

What people often fail to see, and fail to accept, is that their loss changed them. For example, if you got a divorce, you are now single, whether you like it or not. You have a new box to check off on forms: divorced. Or maybe you lost your job. Your identity used to be as an electrician, but if you can't find another job, then who are you now? Can "unemployed" become an identity as much as "electrician" was? What about losing your health? What if you are suddenly restricted to a wheelchair? How does it feel to carry the label, "disabled?"

Since people don't like their new identity, they often get stuck in blame, self-pity, and denial: finding ways to dismiss or minimize their new status.

But there's a better way to identify yourself than married/divorced, employed/unemployed, or able/disabled, etc. You are simply God's child. You are loved by a caring Father who is committed to bringing you to a better place. If you insist on clinging to old identities, you will never be able to receive the new identity, life, and experiences that God has for you.

When a person is able to find their identity apart from other people (relationships), or their associations (work, hobby, health, etc.), we call them "differentiated." They are able to distinguish themselves from whom they know and what they do. If you want to leave exile, differentiation is imperative.

Jesus was differentiated. He found his identity in God alone. He said:
> If I give honor to myself, that honor is worth nothing. The One who gives me honor is my Father... John 8:54, NCV.

Jesus tells us he didn't look to others for affirmation or identity. His worth came from God. In another place, Jesus chided the people of his day on this point saying:

F. Remy Diederich

> You try to get praise from each other, but you do not try to get the praise that comes from the only God. John 5:44, NCV.

In other words, we too often find our worth in what other people have to say about us and not in what God says about us.

Jesus' words show us he was differentiated. He didn't allow himself to be defined by his work, or ministry, or family status. No one could intimidate him because he only listened to what his Father said about him.

When Jesus was baptized a voice came from heaven that said, "This is my Son with whom I am well pleased." That was the only affirmation Jesus needed to hear. He never pandered to the masses seeking their approval. As a result, Jesus was never devastated when people rejected him. Even in his death, he was able to say,
> Father forgive them for they do not know what they are doing. Luke 23:34

Since Jesus found his identity in God, and not people, he wasn't obligated to defend his honor. He didn't need to prove his worth. Revenge wasn't necessary. He was free to forgive.

No matter what has happened to you; no matter what you've lost, you are God's child. For that reason, you are a person of infinite worth and value. That is how you ought to frame yourself and that is the title you should place on your picture. No one can take that away from you.

Return from Exile

What about you?
- Take a look in the mirror. *What, or who, defines you? What frames your identity? What is the label you hang on that picture?*

- *How is it keeping you from returning from exile?*

- *How have you been hurt by what people have said about you in exile?*

- *How have they misjudged you?*

- *How would finding your identity in God alone free you to return from exile?*

Day Thirty-Seven

Reframing God

A scarcity mindset holds God in contempt. Whether you mean to or not, you imply that God is not enough. He is not sufficient for your need.

Several years ago I lamented the life of someone I was counseling. It didn't seem like they would ever climb out of the hole they were in. Their life was a series of tragedy and loss. Then I remembered Psalm 23 where David said of God, "...he restores my soul." It struck me that those words were either true or false. Did I believe God was a restorer of souls or not? I believed he was.

I'm convinced many people stay stuck in exile because of a low view of God. For whatever reason, they don't believe God is a restorer of souls, and they pay the price for it.

Return from Exile

My last recommendation for reframing your exile has to do with choosing to see God as a god of abundance, not scarcity. How do you view God? Do you expect him to show up on your behalf, or do you always assume the worst, that he will leave you high and dry?

Scarcity is about fear. You fear there won't be enough: enough money, enough love, enough time, enough medicine, enough forgiveness: whatever it is you need in life.

Scarcity focuses on what little you have; it's all you'll get, and if you aren't careful you will even lose that.

Scarcity is about walls and locks and secrets and hiding because you can never be too careful to guard your meager holdings.

Abundance is the opposite. Abundance is about hope.

Abundance sees opportunities when others are cutting back and preparing to throw in the towel.

Abundance enables you to be generous even when you have little to spare.

Have you ever noticed how many seeds a tree throws off every year? Literally thousands. One tree sheds enough seeds to create a forest. God has wired abundance and prosperity into his creation. If he's done that for trees, won't he do it for his children?

In the wanderings of the Sinai Wilderness, God's people doubted his goodness. They doubted he would meet their needs. God responded:

> How long will these people treat me with contempt? How long will they refuse to believe in me, in spite of all the signs I have performed among them? Numbers 14:11

A scarcity mindset holds God in contempt. Whether you mean to or not, you imply that God is not enough. He is not sufficient for your need.

Paraphrasing Numbers 14, God responded by saying: *Okay. It's your choice. If you don't think I can help you overcome the obstacles then fine, don't enter the Promised Land.* And in fact, they didn't enter. They wandered in the Sinai Peninsula for forty years.

It didn't have to be that way. They had a choice.

In contrast to their contempt, Abraham trusted God. He believed in a God of abundance: the God of resurrection. Paul wrote that Abraham believed in:

> ...the God who gives life to the dead and calls things that are not as though they were. Against all hope, Abraham in hope believed and so became the father of many nations ...Without weakening in his faith, he faced the fact that his body was as good as dead–since he was about a hundred years old–and that Sarah's womb was also dead. Yet he did not waver through unbelief regarding the promise of God, but was strengthened in his faith and gave glory to God, being fully persuaded that God had power to do what he had promised. This is why "it was credited to him as righteousness." Romans 4:17-22

Return from Exile

We serve the God who gives life to the dead and calls things that are not into being. I know there are exceptions. I know all stories don't end in resurrection and deliverance in this life. But God is a god of abundance. Why not expect and hope for the best? Why not expect something amazing...even if that's an amazing sense of peace and joy in your exile?

Maybe you are in a hopeless place. But did you see what Abraham did? It says... *against all hope, Abraham believed in hope...* and as a result of his hope, he became the father of many nations. His hope enabled him to prosper.

You are not a fool to hope. You are a person of faith.

What about you?
- *Contempt is a strong word. Do you think you've held God in contempt for not delivering you from exile?*

- *What do you think it will take for you to be able to believe God can give you new life?*

Day Thirty-Eight

Necessary Endings

Some people like exile. They like the drama...
they have no intention of returning;
they just hope they can string you along
to stay with them and keep them company.

Our 40-day journey is nearing the end. I hope you are getting your questions answered about what exile is about and how to return from exile.

Today I want to talk about a touchy subject: your fellow travelers. It's touchy because the truth is you might get stuck in exile if you are afraid to distance yourself from them. You see, some people like exile. They like the drama. They like being contrarian. They've never fit in, so being in the desert is their comfort zone. They wouldn't know what to do if life was "normal."

Return from Exile

That's fine. It's their life. But at some point you have to decide if you want to continue on with them or not. You don't want them holding your life hostage.

Your mistake is assuming they want to return from exile. They don't. They like to *talk* about returning. They will make *promises* about returning, but they have no intention of returning; they just hope they can string you along to stay with them and keep them company.

Meanwhile you wait for them. You hope for them. You pray for them. You believe in them...*until you don't*...until it becomes painfully obvious they don't want to leave exile. They never did. Deep down they like playing the victim and letting people feel sorry for them. They thrive on pity, self-pity, and the chaos that surrounds them. They pride themselves on being the outsider. When this realization hits you, you get a sinking feeling as you think about all the time you've wasted on them.

So here's the hard part: you may need to walk away from them if you ever want to return from exile. I know you don't want to do that. Exile is hard enough *with* someone, let alone on your own. Plus, they always lay a guilt trip on you when you mention leaving, compelling you to give them another chance. After all, you are a Christian. Should you really cut them loose?

But seriously, walking away might be the right thing: for you and them. Your sticking with them only enables their self-defeating behavior. And besides, you won't be alone forever. Eventually you'll find other people headed in the same direction you are...healthy people...humble people... people ready to live the new life they discovered in exile.

I think you know what I'm talking about. You know *who* I'm talking about. The question is: will you walk away and return from exile or allow them to lead you in circles through the Wilderness forever? It's your choice.

What about you?
- *Who are the people keeping you trapped in exile?*

- *What steps should you take to separate yourself from them?*

Day Thirty-Nine

Double Blessings

Exile stripped you, but God wants to make your life good again. More than that, he wants to celebrate you...YOU...in all of your weakness and failure.

I mentioned earlier that King David was confident that God restores our soul (Psalm 23). It's interesting to look at how God restored people throughout the Bible.

A common theme relating to restoration in the Bible is that God restored people to a place *better* than before their exile, often with a double blessing. Here are a few examples.
- Naaman's leprous hand "was restored like the flesh of a little child..." 1 Kings 5:1-14.
- God restored Job's fortunes "two-fold." Job 42:10.

- God restored Nebuchadnezzar with "surpassing greatness..." Daniel 4:36,37.
- God spoke through Zechariah that he would restore double to his people. Zechariah 9:11,12.

Is it too much to hope that God might restore double to you as well? Restoring double communicates the exile is at last over, you are fully accepted, and the window of blessing is now wide open to you.

The prophet Isaiah delivered a vivid picture of God's restorative work and double blessing. As you read it below, notice the progression. In the first three verses Isaiah tells of how God will restore the exiles. Then in verse four it's the former exiles who bring restoration to the land. And finally, the newly restored land becomes home to other exiles (strangers and foreigners).

> 1 The Spirit of the Sovereign LORD is on me, because the LORD has anointed me to proclaim good news to the poor. He has sent me to bind up the brokenhearted, to proclaim freedom for the captives and release from darkness for the prisoners,
> 2 to proclaim the year of the LORD's favor and the day of vengeance of our God, to comfort all who mourn,
> 3 and provide for those who grieve in Zion— to bestow on them a crown of beauty instead of ashes, the oil of joy instead of mourning, and a garment of praise instead of a spirit of despair. They will be called oaks of righteousness, a planting of the LORD for the display of his splendor.
> 4 They will rebuild the ancient ruins and restore the places long devastated; they will renew the

ruined cities that have been devastated for generations.
5 Strangers will shepherd your flocks; foreigners will work your fields and vineyards.
6 And you will be called priests of the LORD, you will be named ministers of our God. You will feed on the wealth of nations, and in their riches you will boast.
7 Instead of your shame you will receive a **double portion**, and instead of disgrace you will rejoice in your inheritance. And so you will inherit a **double portion** in your land, and everlasting joy will be yours. Isaiah 61:1-7, (emphasis mine).

God heals us to bring healing. It's a beautiful picture of how God's love flows from him and spreads to all. He is generous to us so that we will be generous to others.

The most famous story of double blessing comes from Jesus' story of The Prodigal Son (Read it in Luke 15:11ff). The shock of that story is that the Prodigal wasn't met with disappointment when he returned home, but celebration.

Just as the father received back his son, God welcomes you back from exile. But the father did more than welcome back his son: he put a robe around his shoulders, a ring on his finger, sandals on his feet, and then threw him a party. That's more than restoration. That's *celebration*, even in spite of his betrayal. His father went above and beyond what existed before in their relationship. God wants to celebrate you in the same way.

But, if you want that kind of celebration, you have to do

what the Prodigal did: receive it. He could have refused it, saying he wasn't worthy. But he stepped into the blessing and took on a new identity in order to live a new life.

What about you?
- *Do you have hope of being restored?*

- *Can you imagine God not only restoring you but giving you a double blessing? Why is that?*

- *Is God trying to bless you now, but you are unwilling to receive it?*

- *Are there any ways that you habitually sabotage God's blessings, meaning that you avoid them, refuse them, or undermine them in some way?*

Be on the look out for God's goodness. Why not assume the best of him?

Day Forty

Goodness and Mercy

I'm confident God not only provides a way to return from exile, but longs to restore and prosper us.

Today marks the end of our 40-day journey in, through, and hopefully out, of exile. Thanks for walking with me over these days as I've sought to help you process the losses, betrayals, setbacks, burn-out, and possible outright rebellion that landed you in exile. I know the shock of waking up far from anything that looks remotely familiar, wondering if you will ever find your way back home.

Let me re-quote Richard Rohr as I close out our time together:
> The soul has many secrets. They are only revealed to those who want them, and are never

completely forced upon us. One of the best-kept secrets, and yet one hidden in plain sight, is that the way up is the way down. Or, if you prefer, the way down is the way up.

In Scripture, we see that the wrestling and wounding of Jacob are necessary for Jacob to become Israel (Genesis 32:26-32), and the death and resurrection of Jesus are necessary to create Christianity. The loss and renewal pattern is so constant and ubiquitous that it should hardly be called a secret at all.

I hope you see by now that loss, or what I've been calling "exile," is not an aberration. It's not random. And it's not something God only uses to punish his people. Loss comes to us all. It's a part of life we should flow with, learn from, and return from to continue on with God's calling on our lives...only as better people.

When I lived on our farm, one of the many things I learned about farm life is that death is as much a part of the farm as was life. You think of a farm as a place with many living animals. But when you are there 24/7, you soon realize death happens all around you. There is a rhythm of life and death. I'd imagine people who work in hospitals experience the same thing.

We live in a sanitized world where we quickly remove pain, suffering, death, or anything that makes us feel uncomfortable. We have lost our ability to suffer, learn patience, grieve and then recover well. As a result we've become shallow, self-absorbed people who get stuck in exile, having no idea how to return.

Return from Exile

But I'm confident God not only provides a way for us to return from exile, but longs to restore and prosper us as well. David was convinced "goodness and mercy" would "follow him all the days of his life" even though he walked through the valley of the shadow of death (Psalm 23).

When my wife and I moved off of our farm, into town, and back into ministry, I was surprised at how quickly the blessings of God came back into our lives. That was in 1997, and they continue today.

One day I was reading through Psalm 31 where it says:
> How great is your goodness that you have stored up for those who fear you that you have given to those who trust you. You do this for all to see. Psalm 31:19, NASB.

I felt like God was speaking to me directly, saying:
> *Remy, you think you wasted seven years of your life. You think the world passed you by and life will never be what you hoped it would be. But all the time you were enduring hardship, I was storing up the goodness you were missing. And now I'm bringing that goodness out of storage for you to enjoy.*

The ministry I enjoy now is far beyond what I ever imagined. Through the ministry of Cedarbrook Church, Arbor Place Treatment Center, my books, and mentoring pastors, I have impacted thousands of people. I don't say that with pride, but humility. I'm humbled at what God has done with someone who thought he was a ministry washout. If you would have told me this would be my life twenty years ago, when I was milking cows, I would have told you to quit smoking that stuff! How was that possible?

But the reality of my time in exile was that it didn't detract from my ministry; it enhanced it because *exile enhanced me.* I came out a different person. A better person. I find it hard to believe God would want any more for me than he wants for you. I have to believe he has goodness stored up for you as well.

My hope in writing for these forty days, and my prayer for you now, is you will experience the fullness of God's goodness to such an extent it will overflow from you and into the life of others. After all, isn't that what God is working into all of us...a generous heart to reveal his goodness to others?

Thanks again for traveling with me. God bless you in your journey. I'd like to leave you with the lyrics to Jason Gray's song, *Nothing is Wasted*:
>The hurt that broke your heart and left you trembling in the dark,
>feeling lost and alone, will tell you hope's a lie.
>But what if every tear you cry will seed the ground where joy will grow?
>
>And nothing is wasted. Nothing is wasted.
>In the hands of our Redeemer. Nothing is wasted.
>
>It's from the deepest wounds that beauty finds a place to bloom and you will see before the end that every broken piece is gathered in the heart of Jesus. And what's lost will be found again.
>
>And nothing is wasted. Nothing is wasted.

In the hands of our Redeemer. Nothing is wasted.

From the ruins. From the ashes. Beauty will rise. From the wreckage. From the darkness. Glory will shine.

My prayer for you: *Father, might the words to this song be a prophecy of hope for my reader. Help them to learn all that you have for them in their loss and that nothing's been wasted. Then, may they return from exile add value the lives of everyone they encounter. Help them to reclaim their life and receive the double-blessing that you have for them. Amen.*

What about you?
- *Do you ever feel like you have wasted years of your life in exile? Why or why not?*

- *How might God redeem your loss in positive ways?*

- *What are the biggest take-aways you've gotten from this journey?*

- *What are your next steps?*

- *Whom do you know that might benefit from receiving this 40-day journey?*

Epilogue

The Desert Prepares You for a Comeback

No matter what your situation is today, no matter how remote, how harsh, how isolated...
God can use it to make you grow and become strong.

Once I came upon the theme of "exile" in the Bible, I started to see it everywhere. For example, I just started a study of Luke's account of Jesus. The last verse in chapter one seems like a "throwaway" verse...a simple statement that wraps up a long chapter. But on second look, I saw another truth about exile.

Luke is talking about John the Baptist:
> ...the child *grew and became strong* in spirit and he *lived in the desert* until he appeared publicly

to Israel. Luke 1:80, (emphasis mine).

Where did John grow and become strong? In church? In seminary? At the university? At a spiritual retreat center? No. *In the desert*...the last place we think good things can happen. Our view of the desert is a place where your strength is drained. But not in God's economy. That's where God makes his greatest investment in you.

No matter what your situation is today, no matter how harsh it is, or how isolated you feel...God can use your exile to make you grow and become strong. It can be the place he prepares you to take your life to the next level so you can return to be a blessing to others. You will no longer be Abram, but Abraham.

Father, help my readers to see their desert as a place where they can grow and become strong. Help them to not limit what you want to do in their lives by their circumstances. Thank you for the good things you have in store for them. Help them to believe you are the God of resurrection.

Please let other people know what you think of this book. Take a moment to leave a review at amazon.com.

Appendix: The Gift of Cancer

In this book I've tried to briefly mention a number of types of exile, whether that's financial, or relational, or health, etc. Many people have experienced the exile of cancer, my sister (Diedre Kaye) being one of them. She wrote a post for her CaringBridge blog that I want to share with you here because it embodies the idea of reframing perfectly. When she was able to call cancer a "gift" I knew that she was on her way out of exile. She stood the test and came out a winner.

One Qualifier

Before I share her thoughts, it's important to acknowledge that, if your life, or the life of a loved one, was ravaged by cancer, then hearing it called a "gift" might be offensive. I understand and appreciate that. Everyone's experience is different. But I'm happy to know that Diedre *gained* something from her cancer experience rather than let it steal from her. I hope her words encourage you. This is what she wrote:

The Gift of Cancer

In reading other blogs, I have seen that maintaining a positive attitude through our journeys is common of the bloggers and their followers. On that note, I have rewritten a common saying on what cancer cannot do to what it can do for us. This saying has been sent to me a couple of times over the past 8 months and they are posted in my office.

> *Cancer is so limited...*
> *It cannot cripple love,*
> *It cannot shatter hope,*
> *It cannot corrode faith,*
> *It cannot destroy peace,*

It cannot kill friendship,
It cannot suppress memories,
It cannot silence courage,
It cannot invade the soul,
It cannot steal eternal life,
It cannot conquer the spirit. – Author unknown

I believe all these statements are true, but I also see that cancer has been a gift in my life. I have chosen not to fight it, and be angry with it, but to recognize its gifts, be grateful for them, and then encourage it to leave my body. So far, it's been a good approach.

I have chosen to rewrite the common cancer phrases in a more positive light. I hope you can understand my position on why I choose to follow this journey:
Cancer can be a gift...
It can expand your love,
It can encourage hope,
It can enhance faith,
It can bring peace,
It can build friendships,
It can make new memories,
It can develop courage,
It can blossom the soul,
It can help me face eternal life,
It can inspire the spirit.

No matter what journey we are following, whether it's a loss of a loved one, a concern for a child, a tragic occurrence, depression, or any disease, we all need to keep the spirit of joy, love and gratitude in our hearts. May we all look for those gifts every day that make us happy. *Diedre Kaye*

Return from Exile

Good Can Come From Even Cancer

It's humbling to me to read Diedre's words when I know she has suffered so much. But I'm grateful because she shows me how you can trust God to make good out of anything, even cancer. It's the ultimate act of worship. Rather than focus and lament over what's been lost, why not focus on what's been gained? There's nothing to gain by cursing your loss, or God, for that matter. It's far better to look for the good that God can bring from it.

Too often I hear people speak as if God owes them a pain-free life. Any pain is fought with bitterness and they resent God for allowing it to visit them. But I haven't read that guarantee anywhere. Where does it say that God owes us anything? The sage, Job, said it best thousands of years ago:

> Naked I came from my mother's womb, and naked I will depart. The LORD gave and the LORD has taken away; may the name of the LORD be praised. Job 1:21

I'm grateful that God is willing to walk with me through my pain and give me eyes to see the silver lining that exists if I look for it. Bitterness only shuts me down and closes me off to all that's good, even the healing I might be longing for. Gratefulness does just the opposite.

I hope you can see the gifts in your life today, especially the gifts that are hiding in your loss.

A Word from the Author

I'm happy to correspond with you through email to answer your questions or receive your thoughts and feedback. I love hearing people's stories and adding to my understanding of exile and restoration.

- Please email me at remydiederich@yahoo.com.
- Follow my author page at F. Remy Diederich on Facebook.
- Read my blog at readingremy.com.

If you would like your church to process this forty-day journey together through sermons and small group study, contact me for a special offer that includes books, free sermons, and study guides.

Remy Diederich
December 2016

p.s. If you would like to offer your pastor a free copy of "Out of Exile," my book directed specifically to the losses that pastors face, send them this link: www.readingremy.com/free

Other books by F. Remy Diederich

Healing the Hurts of Your Past...*a guide to overcoming the pain of shame.* In this practical guide, Remy breaks down what causes our insecurities and shows how they manifest in a variety of self-destructive ways. But unlike most self-help books, Remy goes beyond describing the problem; he offers a solution by clearly helping the reader find their infinite worth from knowing what God did for them through Jesus Christ.

STUCK...*how to overcome anger and reclaim your life.* Anger is natural. It's a God-given gift to process loss. With this positive approach to anger, Remy walks his reader through a deeper understanding of what causes anger and how to process it effectively. This process involves a discussion of grief, loss, and forgiveness. Remy's practical approach enables his reader to work their way through complex life scenarios to free themselves from feeling STUCK in anger.

Out of Exile: *Pastor's Edition.* This book is directed at helping pastors and ministry leaders who have suffered a setback in ministry and are looking to make a comeback. It formed the basis for "Return from Exile.

Acknowledgements:

I've learned so much about loss from my fellow travelers. I'm thankful to my wife, Lisa, for being such a gracious companion through various exiles. It's always so much easier with two than alone. My sister Diedre and her husband, Alexx, have shown great grace under the fire of Diedre's journey through cancer. My mother, Barbara, showed me how to manage the exile of old age and death. Plus there are the many people I walk with daily at both Cedarbrook Church and Arbor Place Treatment Center who have taught me much about God's restorative work in exile.

Friends are made in exile. Here's a shout-out to Jim and Carol Gustafson, Steve and Patricia Gjertsen, Bruce and Cheryl Lyke, Marilyn Gauger, Dave and Ellen Liberto, Steve and Rae Jean Clason. And a special thanks to the Rasmussen family (wherever you are) for encouraging us during our exile, and Jim and Patti Walker for helping us find our way out of exile.

I also want to acknowledge the ministry staff at Cedarbrook Church who work everyday to help people find God in the midst of their brokenness: Sandra Bauman, Sten Carlson, Stephanie Demers, Kris Ann Erickson, Kyle Gunderson, and Christine Thompson.

And finally, my thanks to Jason Brooks who has helped each one of my books become a reality. Without him you wouldn't be reading this book.

About the Author

F. Remy Diederich is the founding and lead pastor of Cedarbrook Church in Menomonie, Wisconsin. He consults at Arbor Place Treatment Center, working with clients to understand how God can be a part of their recovery process. You can correspond with him at remydiederich@yahoo.com.

[1] From Dictionary.com

[2] Dallas Willard, The Divine Conspiracy, p. 21

[3] The other three primary losses are: exposed weaknesses, irritating behavior, and embarrassing behavior.

[4] Some people have mentioned to me that God has also used musicians to bring them comfort in exile.

[5] To sign up for Rohr's daily devotional visit: www.cac.org

[6] I'm still not sure what was wrong. The latest thought is Seasonal Affectiveness Disorder, or S.A.D.

[7] First introduced by Swiss psychiatrist Elisabeth Kübler-Ross in her 1969 book, *On Death and Dying*.

[8] Segerstrom, S.C., Stanton, A.L., Alden, L.E., & Shortridge, B.E. (2003). A multidimensional structure for repetitive thought: What's on your mind, and how, and how much? Journal of Personality and Social Psychology, 85, 909-921.

[9] From Richard Rohr's Daily Mediation: The Freedom of Not Knowing, Meditation 32 of 52 at cac.org.

[10] See Acts 22:3-16

[11] Read Judges 14-16

[12] The Secrets of Leadership, TIME magazine, Jul. 21, 2008

[13] Cries from the Heart, Stories of Struggle and Hope, Johann Christoph Arnold.

Made in the USA
Middletown, DE
22 August 2017